The Entitlement-Free CHILD

Raising Confident and Responsible Kids
in a "Me, Mine, Now!" Culture

The
Entitlement-Free
CHILD

Karen Deerwester

SOURCEBOOKS, INC.®
NAPERVILLE, ILLINOIS

Published by Sourcebooks, Inc.
P.O. Box 4410, Naperville, Illinois 60567–4410
(630) 961–3900
Fax: (630) 961–2168
www.sourcebooks.com

Library of Congress Cataloging-in-Publication Data

Deerwester, Karen.
  The entitlement-free child : raising confident and responsible kids in a "me, mine, now!" culture / Karen Deerwester.
    p. cm.
  Includes index.
  1. Parenting. 2. Child rearing. 3. Parent and child. I. Title.
  HQ755.8.D424 2008
  649'.7—dc22

                    2008034038

Printed and bound in the United States of America.
VP 10 9 8 7 6 5 4 3 2 1

*To all the parents who trust that doing the right thing today
makes for a better tomorrow...
and especially to Jeremy, Ioana, and Landen Giani Good*

CONTENTS

One-Size Parenting Doesn't Fit All
Practice, Practice, Practice

PART II: ENTITLEMENT-FREE STRATEGIES FOR EVERYDAY SITUATIONS

ACKNOWLEDGMENTS

A book is started long before you sit at the computer and type the first words. It may start in childhood when something is imprinted in your heart to be retrieved decades later. Or when something happens that mysteriously upends your life, and writing the book collects the pieces back together in a new way. For me, this book isn't just about parenting; it's about learning to live, communicate, and respect myself and others. On this most personal level, I thank my parents, David, Richard, Joan, and Paula for being behind me and at my side through easy times and difficult times.

The topic of this book arose unknowingly from Po Bronson and Jeff Zaslow, who respectively wrote articles on praise and entitlement for *New York Magazine* and the *Wall Street Journal*. These articles prompted my ongoing discussion with Sourcebooks editorial manager Peter Lynch, whom I credit with finding the perfect format for me to enter into a discussion of entitlement and parenting. From there, my no-one-else-can-do-what-she-does editor, Sara Appino, rallied with the tireless precision of a word surgeon to save what should be saved, repair what needed fixing, and make space for essential improvements. I also thank the awesome publicists at Sourcebooks, especially Emily Mullen, for their help getting my books noticed. This book could not have been written anywhere but at Sourcebooks.

Of course, it was the parenting questions that brought this book to paper. I thank all the parents who search for wisdom, sanity, and grace to love and guide their children—especially the parents from the Ruth & Edward Taubman Early Childhood Center at B'nai Torah Congregation in Boca Raton. These parents transformed my well-intentioned advice into something useful for real-life situations. I am grateful to them for giving me an authentic connection to family life.

The final book is distilled from millions of words over thousands of hours. No one who knows me escaped a discussion of entitlement while I was working on this book. I thank all of you for your patience and insight, especially the following professionals, parents, and friends for your individual recommendations: Vicki McCash Brennan from *South Florida Parenting Magazine*, Dr. Timothy Leistner, Barb Pickle, Adena Shriner, Ellyn Laub, Marney Tokar, Nadine Mensch, Aaryn Gottesfeld, Amy Weissman, Rabbi David Steinhardt, Rabbi David and Stephanie Englander, Louise Goldberg, Rich Foss, Ali Menzer, Adele Wessblatt, Leesa Parker, Daniel Parker, Leslie Viselman, Elyssa Stark, Beth Goldstein, Nancy Goldstein, Felice Brodis, Marci Hirsch, Debbie Fried, Sharon Shear, Sheri Zemel, Hilary Silberfarb, Tracy Gindea, Mara Maklan, Dana Gaines, Staci Zellen, Laurie Hill, Scott Ferguson, Liza Muschett, Kasey Bedard, Ellen Munnelly, Neeta Rancourt, and Lynn and Heather Good. You were the safety net that caught me as I tried to say things better. Thank you all.

PART I

The Entitlement-Free Advantage

Parents, everywhere and always, want the best for their children—as they should. They want health, wealth, and happiness, and a little extra of each just in case. This book encourages you to give your children everything they need. It shows you how to raise an entitlement-free child, one who appreciates what he has and respects the needs of others. It also steers you around the pitfalls of entitlement—*Me! Mine! Now!*

The upcoming chapters will help you look beneath the surface of most parenting predicaments and find the assumptions about entitlement. You'll learn how to recognize entitlement behavior early, long before the birthday limos and other extravagances. Entitlement-free living is a choice parents make daily in ordinary family situations. By starting in early childhood with the goal of raising an entitlement-free child, you won't have to undo negative habits years later.

The entitlement child gets everything he asks for...now. He can't wait. A parent saying no doesn't mean no; it means "Maybe, if you keep bugging me" or "I don't really want to, but..." The entitlement child doesn't accept "enough" because he's afraid he might miss out on "more." Driven by immediate gratification, the entitlement child gets what he wants; he just doesn't get what he needs. He gets what he wants today but is unsatisfied tomorrow. His happiness is temporary and conditional.

The entitlement-free child, on the other hand, gets much more. He trusts that his needs will be met, because he has learned that he can count on other people today and tomorrow. Life is okay even when he is frustrated, confused, or upset. He has skills. The entitlement-free child learns to see things from another's point of view, accept limits from others, and delay personal gratification, and he can handle age-appropriate problems. He is thoughtful and resourceful.

Everyone has a little entitlement in them. Children, in particular, can't possibly know that entitlement, like the too-good-to-be-true candy cottage in a fairy tale, isn't good for them—but instead will give them a giant tummy ache. An entitlement childhood is a lonely and scary place for children. Parenthood is full of uncertainty too. The entitlement-free parenting advantage is that *you* can know what is enough— better than your children, better than the toy-touting experts, and better than the fast-pedaling Joneses.

In Part II, you'll find practical strategies to guide you through confusing parenting situations in a world of quick fixes and instant gratification. You'll learn how and when to say no, how and when to praise, how and when to handle age-appropriate challenges, and how to set reasonable expectations with unconditional love. Entitlement or entitlement-free? You have a choice. This book helps you to make the choice that gives your child the very best—always.

1

UNDERSTANDING THE ENTITLEMENT CHILD

The world of entitlement wasn't created in a day. It took decades of consumerism and wealth, of superkids, supersized egos, and hypervigilant parents to amp up to current levels of entitlement behavior. The Entitlement Generation is typically defined as men and women born between 1979 and 1994. This new cultural force drew significant attention in the last few years as Florida State University (2005) and others reported that entitlement kids have grown up and entered the workforce with an unprecedented give-it-to-me-now attitude. One career counseling firm described them as poorly prepared and out of touch. Now, with the so-called Entitlement Generation entering parenthood, the entitlement issues are increasing. New parents need a way to distinguish parenting myths from parenting reality. But it isn't just the Entitlement Generation who needs an effective response to entitlement trends; it's everyone raising children today.

The entitlement child is the one you see in the grocery store cart opening six different packages of food because nothing tastes good. The entitlement child is the child at someone else's birthday party running away with the presents or talking about the best gift from her party. The entitlement child is the child who unilaterally rules at home or in public. She decides what's for dinner and when it's time to leave an activity. Life is about *her.*

Entitlement children are children who have learned from experience that they will get what they want if they demand loud enough or insist long enough. They might accomplish this with irresistible charm or with forceful persistence. Either way, not only do they know how to get their way, they expect it. The problem lies in the nature of that expectation—"Me! Mine! Now!"—without regard to anything or anyone else.

Entitlement isn't a problem because a child seeks immediate gratification of all her desires—that's normal. The problem occurs when parents are confused about how to respond to childhood demands. Entitlement becomes a problem shared by all parents when outside pressures start to outweigh and over-whelm parental decision making. You know your child doesn't *need* designer clothes to wear to preschool, but you naturally want your child to fit in. You know your child has more toys at three years old than most children have in a lifetime, but what kind of parent doesn't buy new toys for birthdays…and holidays and on vacations and, and, and? If only the rest of the world would come to its senses, it would be much easier to stop the insanity.

The University of Minnesota Birthdays Without Pressure Project confirms the pressure on parents is real. The website reports that 71 percent of parents claim that parties in their community cost too much and kids receive too many pres-ents. Fifty-eight percent say they worry that their parties are not as good as their neighbors'. Parents choosing to resist community trends are not only swimming against a tidal wave of entitlement and consumerism, they also face the internal struggle of "Why not *my* child?" The inner conviction to say no is overruled by outside influences. Unfortunately, the consequences of giving in put children at risk.

The American Psychological Association Task Force on Advertising and Children (2004) reminds parents that children under the age of eight lack the cognitive skills to manage the persuasive powers of advertising. Children need adult protection from misleading images. Young children don't know the difference between needs and wants; they believe it when someone on television tells them they *need* the newest hot item, a cereal will make them happy, or that a $200 toy is affordable to everyone watching. A few isolated incidents may be harmless, but child advocates like the Campaign for a Commercial-Free Childhood are now asking for legislation to address the growing influence of media on children.

This is not your parents' consumer culture. The American Academy of Pediatrics policy statement on "Children, Adolescence, and Advertising" (2006) notes the high-stake gains from winning over younger consumers—hundreds of billions of spending dollars. Parents are being challenged to withstand a groundswell of sophisticated and subtle pressure to buy more products and experiences that promise to enhance their children's happiness and success. And children are being used as pawns in the spending game. In the past, the parent giving in was the exception; now, the parent saying no stands alone.

Unfortunately, all that buying and giving creates an entitlement child unprepared for age-appropriate experiences. These are the children who believe they are treated unfairly if they receive a less-than-perfect grade, even though they never turned in their homework. These same children struggle with friendships because they believe their needs are more important than someone else's. Children who are overprotected and overindulged become young adults who rely on their helicopter parents to complete their college applications and negotiate health benefits with their future employers. They are the interns who act like CEOs on their first day of work. Entitlement children thrive, but only in the bubble of their own perfection.

WHAT IS ENTITLEMENT?

Entitlement wasn't always a bad thing. It insured basic rights and privileges. Entitlement social programs, for example, are based on a shared belief that citizens are entitled to certain services regardless of limiting conditions or exceptions. This concept of entitlement guarantees that certain opportunities are open to everyone. Entitlement without responsibility, however, opens the door to unexpected problems. Children are entitled to quality education, but a quality education is possible only when students come to school and agree to certain tasks. Children learn more when more is expected of them and when they are invested in learning. Balance is essential. Otherwise one person's "right" becomes another person's obligation. A "you owe me" attitude eventually fails.

Children have rights, in society and in families. All parents should encourage children to reach their fullest potential. Children should strive to realize their greatest dreams and absolutely should be valued as human beings. Children should expect success, but that expectation must also include a sense of responsibility for themselves and for their actions. Being good at something takes time, talent, and practice. Parents can help, teach, comfort, lead, and follow, but they cannot live their children's lives or learn their children's lessons.

Entitlement children are not defined here as those with healthy self-respect and a gracious respect for others. Entitlement behavior is negative when it is defined by a Me-Mine-Now attitude and Me-Mine-Now actions. When entitlement becomes a relentless demand for immediate gratification

("Me! Mine! Now!"), it hurts the child and the child's ability to reach her fullest potential. The entitlement child is handicapped by a lack of self-control, the inability to work with others, and by short-sighted problem solving.

Children learn at a young age how to control emotions, defer gratification, make good decisions, care about the consequences of their choices, and create solutions that account for the needs of others—or not. Sometimes they learn too late that the strategies that worked for them at home do not work with friends, coworkers, and spouses. Or worse, the squeaky wheel gets rewarded or money buys exemptions to the rules. The world tries to accommodate the inappropriate behavior until it becomes totally unbearable. Everyone hopes that someone else will solve the problem. Eventually everyone is frustrated—parents, schools, businesses, sports fans, travelers, everyone. The imperative is more urgent now than ever to respond to inappropriate entitlement behavior. But getting angry about entitlement isn't effective.

Change doesn't begin with statements that focus on "those bratty kids" or "those selfish parents." Indignation over entitlement won't produce an entitlement-free world. Humiliating or shaming people into entitlement-free behavior is guaranteed to miss the mark. No one is entitled to an entitlement-free world, though we agree it's a better place to be.

Uniting together will change entitlement individualism. Most parents can sympathize with the pressure to do more, buy more, and give in just one more time. Change begins with a sympathetic understanding of the enticements of entitlement and the understanding that entitlement parenting doesn't work. Each parent making entitlement-free choices can begin to create a new cultural climate of respect.

EMOTIONS AND IMPULSES

Entitlement children are ruled by their impulses. From a very young age, all children experience frustration, anger, sadness, disappointment, confusion, and uncertainty, not to mention hundreds of other emotions. The entitlement child never learns how to handle negative emotions, because negative emotions are perceived to be unnecessary or detrimental to the child's well-being. The sources of the negative emotions are quickly removed, so the child is never in a state of discomfort long enough to discover how to think and feel at the same time. She is not an active participant in her own emotional life learning in age-appropriate increments—if I'm frustrated, I can try a different way; if I'm too angry to speak, I can find a place to calm down; if something isn't fair, I can find a way to make it better. Instead adults rescue the entitlement child—if she's bored and wants to leave the store, the rest of the family follows; if she doesn't like what's served for dinner, she gets a special meal; if she forgets her favorite toy at Grandma's house, Dad drops everything and drives back to get it.

Emotions become the master of the child. I want—I need. The child falls apart when things don't go the way she wants. The child acts out in destructive ways. Initially, the entitlement child hits, pouts, screams, or cries, all without any positive resolution. With age and experience, the child discovers how to use her emotions to control others ("Give me my way or I will make your life impossible").

THE PARENTAL DILEMMA

The difference between entitlement parenting and entitlement-free parenting is the parent's problem-solving strategy. Well-meaning parents see a child struggling and suffering. In a misguided attempt to help, they try to make the problem go away. Parents need to find the right balance between dependence and independence, and empathize with the child while simultaneously having the strength to fearlessly acknowledge difficult emotions. Only then can the parent lead the child through difficult moments.

The entitlement-free parent in the store looks for ways to engage the bored child while the rest of the family finishes what they came to do. The entitlement-free child at the dinner table discovers that some foods aren't their favorites but they're okay to eat, because other people really enjoy them. And the child with the forgotten toy survives a time of sadness and disappointment with caring hugs and is happily reunited with her toy tomorrow or next week.

Negative emotions are like relentless mobsters collecting payola. If you try to hush them up, they will own you. But if you call them out into the open and face them, you will successfully stand in your own power. Children need someone smarter and stronger to face down scary emotions.

Emotional struggles are unavoidable as children grow. They actually define the journey of becoming a person. Because she does not have to face these emotional struggles, the entitlement child actually misses this opportunity to learn and grow. The entitlement child cannot respond successfully to ordinary age-appropriate challenges. Regrettably, she never builds the emotional foundation that will prepare her to conquer any obstacles in her life. The entitlement child thrives in a protective bubble but lacks the flexibility and resilience to face an unpredictable future. This is the child who never loses at Chutes and Ladders, or whose parents wait indefinitely for her to be ready to leave the playground.

Children often ask for things that are not good for them or are not reasonable at the moment. They don't understand why they can't walk around airplanes in flight. They believe they are ready to care for a puppy, when they can't remember to pick up their socks. They try to bathe the baby when no one is watching. Parents inevitably ask things of children that are unpleasant. Sometimes they must take children to the doctor for painful procedures. Sometimes parents go to work when their children don't want to say good-bye. In choices large and small, parents make decisions that children do not understand or do not choose for themselves. Guilt is inevitable as parents face the unforeseen limitations of parenthood. And irrational guilt leads to irrational expectations.

You can't always make your child happy. Parents *do* feel worse than the children when they have to say no. But if you give your child everything she wants and magically erase all problems, your child will be trapped in an entitlement world. The entitlement child never acquires the skills to maneuver around life's obstacles. Even worse, the entitlement child never discovers her inner resourcefulness or potential.

FROM GUILT TO FEAR

Guilt-driven parenting is fueled by irrational expectations. Do you believe it's your job to give your child a happy and memorable childhood, perfect parents, and a perfect world? What if you make a mistake? What if your child has a harder time in school or making friends because of something you do? What if you cannot give your child the same advantages in life that other children have? Children need parents—as imperfect as they happen to be. Perfect parents do not raise perfect kids; they raise children who fear not being good enough.

The entitlement child lives in an artificial world where difficulties never happen. Yet she sees the contradiction every day—those difficult emotions and age-appropriate struggles always return. New baby brothers are brought home. She can't run as fast or as far as someone at school. Someone she likes doesn't like her. Without age-appropriate skills for handling difficult emotions, the entitlement child lives in fear. She isn't sure that others can and will help her if she has a problem, and she questions her own ability to face challenges triumphantly. She screams for attention—ME! She fights for what she thinks she needs—MINE! And she frantically stakes her claim—NOW!

The entitlement child behaves this way because underneath her bravado is relentless uncertainty. Her emotions are unsettling. The rules are unpredictable. Every time the people around her scramble to keep her happy, she witnesses her own power to create chaos in the world. Imagine a child who can make adults jump through hoops in desperation or push adults into an emotional frenzy. That's outright scary to a little person who's counting on others to be her anchor in a storm. The adults reinforce rather than alleviate the underlying panic. Behind the entitlement child's demands for Me-Mine-Now is anxiety:

- *If I don't get what I want now, it won't be there for me later.*
- *If you get yours before me, you might take too much.*
- *If I wait, it won't be the same or feel as good.*
- *What if you have something I don't have?*
- *What if what you have is better than what I have?*

TWO-YEAR-OLD ENTITLEMENT THINKING

Two-year-olds are perfect examples of entitlement thinkers. When a child is in that feisty stage called the "terrible-terrific twos" (whether she's eighteen months or three years old), she is adamant about wanting her way…now. When you say no (or "Time for bed," or say her favorite shirt is in the laundry), she cannot fathom why you are thwarting her perfect plan. She explodes with tantrums and meltdowns. Sometimes she'll even fight a positively good idea just because it's your idea and not hers. Notice the persuasiveness of asking a two-year-old not to do something, like "Don't sit in this chair," when you really want her to sit in the chair. A two-year-old lacks the reasoning skills and the self-control to wait or to calmly manage a problem. Her entire agenda is to establish personal autonomy.

Entitlement behaviors are normal in two-year-olds. Little two-year-olds have also been known to reemerge unexpectedly in older children and in fully grown adults. That's normal too. Anyone can slip into entitlement behavior on a bad day when neediness consumes rationality. Entitlement is a world of fear, competition for scarcity, and every man for himself. Everyone is perched to protect possessions and position, just like these classic two-year-old demands:

- *I see candy. I want candy now, not after dinner.*
- *I see your toy. I like my toy better, but I still want yours too.*
- *I want to play inside. I want to play outside. I want both at the same time!*
- *I don't want to go to sleep, ever. I can fight to keep myself awake.*
- *I don't believe tomorrow will be just like today. I want it NOW!*

In time, however, two-year-olds grow, ideally learning the problem-solving skills and the communication skills to manage difficult emotions. They progress out of entitlement thinking. They come to believe the world is a safe place. They discover there's a place for them in the world.

With your help, your two-year-old grows into an entitlement-free child able to be both assertive and respectful. Words and helpfulness replace tantrums and whining as effective communication. You and your child move together in a dance between dependence and independence, not too fast and not too slow, until your child is ready to take the lead. Entitlement thinking is a stage in development, not a place you want to get stuck for too long.

NEVER ENOUGH

Parenting would be so much easier if there were a chart for how much is enough: a kindergartner needs two and a half hours of extracurricular activities per week; birthday gifts for four-year-old classmates should not exceed twenty-five dollars; and six-year-olds can manage three projects before becoming apathetic and careless. Unfortunately, no one can quantify "enough" across the board. Each child is an individual, with individual strengths and interests. Each child has different abilities and motivations, and all children do not need the same things or the same experiences. One child may have a collection of hundreds of cars, dolls, or dinosaurs. This child meticulously studies and appreciates every piece in the collection while another child grows bored after the third one. This other child might truly treasure one object. For one child, one is enough; for another, one hundred is just right. For those who prefer open spaces and imagination to toys, none is the right number.

A perfect childhood is not made up of a certain number of toys, books, outfits, and family vacations. You can give your child the best-researched, state-of-the-art educational toys, or you can give your child a pile of dirt and giant cardboard box—either one might be enough for your child. You know how much is enough by observing *your* child. In general, if your child appreciates what is hers, values what is hers, age-appropriately cares for what is hers, and shows respect for what belongs to others, your child isn't suffering from over-indulgence. If you're worried, though, look for these signs of potential excess:

- Does your child beg for new toys and then discard them quickly?
- Does your child focus more on quantity than on the actual object?
- Does your child lose things haphazardly and never miss them?
- Does your child know how to handle objects with care?
- Does your child grow bored quickly with what she has?
- Does your child measure her things against what others have?
- Does your child place more emphasis on things than on people?

Your child is forming lifelong attitudes about "enough" by as young as two and three years old. The entitlement child never learns the difference between needs and wants and never learns that ownership has responsibility. These may sound like complex concepts for two- and three-year-olds, but they aren't.

A child learns to be entitlement-free in ordinary situations like accidentally breaking a favorite toy. The entitlement parent rushes out to replace the toy. The entitlement-free parent might say something neutral, like, "Oops, you broke your toy. It won't be the same now." In this case, the child hears the consequence of her action: the toy is broken. There are many entitlement-free problem-solving strategies that can follow: show the child how to play with the broken toy in a different way, try to repair the toy, replace it when it's convenient to do so, or find something else to play with. Each possible solution teaches something important to the child: that ownership has responsibility and possessions have value.

QUICK FIXES

Parenting is filled with quick fixes that take care of the moment but don't solve the problem; these are times when you're buying yourself time. You never intended to live by the quick fix. Your child sleeps in your bed tonight but not tomorrow. Your child eats chocolate before breakfast, just this time. Or this is the last time you buy another stuffed animal to quiet a tantrum. You are hoping against all reason that the problem will simply go away. These are all times of giving in, not because you want to or because you believe in your decision, but because you just don't have the energy to do otherwise. All parents have these moments, because they are human.

Before you know it, the quick fixes start to define your parenting style, creating a spiral of entitlement. Your child starts to feel entitled to an immediate solution. Pretty soon, you're not just giving in, you're giving up. You are exhausted, frustrated, and hopeless. Your child's sense of entitlement fuels more parenting panic, which escalates to the next quick fix. When you feel the frenzy to fix your child's unhappiness, you grab for the first solution you see. There's no time to think. You feel like a person being swallowed in quicksand. As every quick fix falls short, you find yourself sinking deeper and deeper.

More often than not, you've probably tried other ways, and they just don't work with your child. You've told, asked, threatened, or repeated hundreds of times, and your child isn't listening. What else can you do? First, understand that real-world parenting often comes into sharp conflict with our image of parenting. For example, when you tell children something, they don't "get it" immediately. They don't hear the rules once and comply evermore. You may do everything "right," and your child will continue to test your sincerity, still make poor choices, and still struggle with maturity. In the real world, it takes a long time to become mature.

The entitlement-free strategies in the upcoming chapters will guide you through the numerous daily parenting situations that confuse you and derail you. You will see that the quick fix distracts you from a more effective goal. You will learn to appreciate your child's abilities and to create positive environments in which your child may grow and thrive. You will understand the value of mistakes, which allow your child to practice skills in a variety of settings under a variety of conditions. Learning takes time, even for the brightest of children.

ENTITLEMENT BURNOUT

Learning takes time for parents too. It would be so much easier if you could buy good parenting in a kit, watch the demo, follow the directions, and voilà...great kids! Hire someone else to do the dirty work. Buy the right experiences. Wear the right clothes. Make it look easy. Never let 'em see you sweat.

There are countless resources to help you become the parent you want to be and raise the child you want to see. But there are no armchair parents. Parenting require hands-on, heart-in, hold-your-breath relationships. Children are not raised by books, kits, or objective observers; they are raised by people who love them. You and your child are emotionally connected, through better and worse. Your child learns as much from the hard times as from the good.

Entitlement parents forget to pace themselves for the parenting marathon. They fly out of the gate fully committed to being great parents and burn out long before middle school. By the time their children are school-age, the parents are too tired of fighting over homework to find a better way now or too worn down to say no to that new iPhone. Entitlement parents want to have it all and do it all. But choices are inevitable. In an effort to keep everyone happy or to keep the peace, they try to avoid age-appropriate struggles. Rather than face the struggle of engaging the child in an activity that requires effort (like homework), the parent complains to the teacher about the unfairness of the grades or about a conflict between the assignment and extracurricular activities. The entitlement parent works twice as hard avoiding the problem, but the problem doesn't go away. Hello, burnout!

It takes practice to balance the needs of the child with the needs of the family. Entitlement-free practice starts when children are young, when the challenges are smaller. Yes, your two- or three-year-old can learn to put her toys away, because it saves someone else the trouble. She can send thank-you notes even if she doesn't want to, because it's considerate. The entitlement-free parent learns to choose what's best for each child at each new stage and conserves energy for the parenting long run.

NO EXCUSES

Some might say we are raising our kids in an entitlement world of "shop till you drop" and trophy spouses, of narcissism and materialism, of fast food and fast-track kids. This is simply the world we live in now. But there are no excuses for entitlement when it comes to kids. Children thrive in a slow world where there's time to think and time to feel, time to love and time to learn. Entitlement takes shortcuts past the lessons to get to the prize, skipping over experience and effort as if they are irrelevant.

The lessons of childhood cannot be skipped—not without paying a price. The price of entitlement is obvious: People don't like each other anymore. Common courtesies are lost. Social pressure, stress, and fear take the stakes higher and higher. And ultimately, the children lose. They lose the ability to master ordinary challenges. They are blind to other people's needs and interests. And they live in carefully constructed lives that limit their potential. But you can stop it, in your home and in your family. You can make a difference in the life of the child who believes in you. Entitlement-free thinking gives you back your power to make good choices for your family. Sure, sometimes you'll look foolish, and sometimes you'll change your mind. But most times, you'll breathe easier, because solid ground feels a whole lot better than quicksand.

Your child is the ultimate winner, because no one can take away what an entitlement-free child wins. She grows into an adult, knowing that "needs" are not things, that people are not interchangeable, and that she has something valuable to give to make the world a better place.

2

THE ENTITLEMENT-
FREE CHILD

The entitlement-free child is taught from an early age that he matters, that other people matter, and that the two go hand in hand. He is an individual with personal strengths and weaknesses who does not have to be exactly like anyone else, and he understands that his weaknesses are not personal flaws. He is also part of something bigger than himself—a family, a school, a team, a neighborhood. He is the child who is happy at birthday parties even if all the presents aren't for him. You might see him at the park helping another child find a lost stuffed animal. And he is the child who may not be happy when it's time to get off the carousel but still walks on his own two feet.

The entitlement-free child is given the skills to confidently maneuver through age-appropriate situations by parents who continually balance dependence and independence. He can depend on strong, reliable parents who give him a solid foundation from which to grow and who continually teach him to think and act on his own. His parents learn, day by day, when to hold on and when to let go.

YOUR CHILD IS SPECIAL

Mr. Rogers, the soft-spoken advocate for children and self-esteem, was right—your child is special…absolutely and unconditionally. Healthy self-esteem is not self-centered and does not lead to increased entitlement behavior, though recent articles in the *Wall Street Journal* have suggested otherwise. Every child is born with unique strengths, a personal style, and specific interests that influence everything he does. It's important to know what your child likes and dislikes, what is easy for your child and what is difficult, what calms your child and what pushes his buttons, what inspires his curiosity and what tests his patience. The more you appreciate your child's individuality, the easier it will be to trust your child's ability and guide his journey to independence.

A celebration of your child's uniqueness requires unconditional love, love for *this* child. Not some perfect child who's adorable and precocious on a sitcom or a movie. *This* child, who spills his milk. *This* child, who is afraid of the doctor. *This* child, who cries when the teacher corrects his behavior. Unconditional love is love despite mistakes and shortcomings—it is not a justification to overprotect. The entitlement-free parent realistically sees what the child still needs to learn. And then, without fear or humiliation, the entitlement-free parent helps the child to grow.

LOVE AND GUIDANCE

The entitlement-free child is loved and is learning. Love provides the security and the safety to manage the uncertainty of change, of learning. Entitlement-free parents combine love and guidance, because children need both. The entitlement-free

---

Jeffrey Zaslow, "Blame It on Mr. Rogers: Why Young Adults Feel So Entitled," *Wall Street Journal,* July 5, 2007, and "The Entitlement Epidemic: Who's Really To Blame," *Wall Street Journal,* July 19, 2007.

child, like Max in the children's classic *Where the Wild Things Are,* tests limits and boundaries. He then discovers he can't always get his way. But in the end, love (his dinner) is always warm and waiting.

Parenting styles strongly affect children's levels of compliance and sense of competence. Decades of research, from Diane Baumrind in the 1960s to the *Encyclopedia on Early Childhood Development* in 2007, supports the theory that an authoritative parenting style is more beneficial to child development than an authoritarian or permissive parenting style. Entitlement-free parents strive to be authoritative parents. As you read the following description, you can think about your own style.

Authoritarian parents adopt a one-way power relationship of parent-in-charge and child-in-compliance. For example, when a three-year-old child asks why he has to go to his weekly swimming lesson, the authoritarian parent yells, "Because I said so!" The permissive style of parenting takes the focus off the power relationship and emphasizes nurturing the child, but it does not balance that with appropriate limit setting. So, in the same example, the permissive parent may decide it would be better to stop the lesson altogether. An authoritative parenting style, however, accepts that parent-child relationships are two-way interactions with the parent sometimes leading the child, but also sometimes following the child's lead. The authoritative style strives to balance "parent demandingness" and "parent responsiveness." When the authoritative parent's three-year-old protests his swimming lesson, the parent comforts the child and reassures him that he will be okay, but says he must learn to swim. Then, after a few swimming lessons, the child begins to feel more comfortable, and his fear is transformed into confidence. The authoritative parent combines love and respect, independence and problem solving, rules and reasons. Only the authoritative style facilitates raising an entitlement-free child, because it both honors the child's autonomy and teaches respect for other people's points of view.

The interplay between love and guidance becomes pivotal in day-to-day parenting situations that contribute to raising an entitlement-free child. In the upcoming sections, love and guidance are the foundation for the entitlement-free child to:

- manage minor obstacles
- learn important time concepts
- acquire developmental skills through play
- cultivate resilience through humor and optimism
- rise to meet age-appropriate expectations
- gain a sense of security from predictable boundaries
- honor the value of rules (learn how to live with others less stressfully)

THE FOUNDATION OF AN ENTITLEMENT-FREE CHILD

Effort

Children are not deterred by obstacles. They stand up, time and again, learning to walk. They return relentlessly to a locked cabinet. They try and try again, whether it's puzzles or chopsticks, riding a bike or reading a story. They are not surprised that some things take time to master. "Effort" is not a bad word for kids—and an understanding that something good will come from something difficult is essential to raising an entitlement-free child.

Explain to your child the invisible effort that's behind the things he takes for granted every day: food that appears in drive-through windows had to be cooked by someone (not to mention grown by someone else and transported there by someone else), and money that is taken out of the ATM has to be earned. Your child wants to know how things work and why. Curiosity inspires effort, as effort inspires curiosity.

The entitlement-free child conquers small frustrations with your help. Don't give up or give in just because your child is discouraged. Children, like grown-ups, deal with frustration in individual ways; some plow their way through with physical determination, others manage better with reassuring conversations, while others need a hug and gentle coaxing. Help your child find a winning strategy to cut through the particular problems he faces.

1. Identify your child's strengths that can help him in this situation. Effort is more exhausting when you approach it from weaknesses. What does your child already have to help him to be successful? A love of books or music, for example, can ease a rocky adjustment to a new school.

2. Convert strengths into practical skills that help him over life's hurdles. For example, if your child is a rambunctious future stuntman, emulating a favorite movie hero can help him learn more appropriate social skills. Learn to speak "kid talk" without elaborate rationale: "Po, the Kung Fu Panda, found the secret is within. Can you find your inner strength?"

3. Encourage him by noticing small successes and letting him see the light at the end of the tunnel. Children give up because they can't see the big picture. Your child's effort is worthwhile once he realizes that last month, or last week, he couldn't do what he can do now.

Your love and guidance give your child the support and encouragement he needs. In Chapters 4 through 10, you'll find many more examples of ways to guide your child through minor difficulties.

Create an environment where effort is valued. To a child who is discovering the ways of the world, process is more important than product. How you do something is as important as getting it done. Help your child notice *how* things get done.

- How long does it take to bake cookies?
- How many things can he do while sitting in a waiting room?
- How is a scribble different from a love note?
- When does batting practice help in hitting the ball, and at what point does he get tired?
- How long did it take his friends to learn to tie their shoes? How about his brother or his grandmother?
- How does he know when a puzzle is too easy for him, and how long would it take him to do a new puzzle quickly?
- How does it happen that he thinks he's cleaned up his toys only to find a few extras standing somewhere perfectly obvious?

Doing things well takes time and practice. Sometimes effort is fun. You'll be surprised that your attention to details leads to your child's improved focus and concentration.

Time Management

One important reason why a two-year-old struggles with entitlement thinking is because two-year-olds, as well as most preschoolers, do not rationally comprehend the concept of time. Your child isn't trying to drive you crazy when he asks for the tenth time, "Are we there yet?" To him, it really does feel like he's been trapped in that car seat for eternity.

The way your child relates to time will affect his sense of entitlement. The entitlement-free child learns about time from external points of reference: watch the timer, see Mommy waiting, count the stop signs, read the street numbers. The entitlement child learns impatience in his own isolated world, distracted by a DVD to make the car ride as painless as possible.

The entitlement two-year-old grows into an entitlement-free child by learning age-appropriate time-management strategies. Time concepts are easy when they are made concrete. Before DVD players, even grown-ups looked for ways to pass the time on long car trips and counted bottles of beer on the wall. Entitlement-free parents teach their children strategies to control their bodies and develop patience as they learn to manage time. You'll find examples in the upcoming chapters—from getting out of the house in the morning to getting into bed at night, from taking time to nurture genuine friendships to learning there's a time and place for everything. Young children maneuver better with sequences of events that frame the more abstract concepts of minute, day, or week.

A school day is a sequence of activities: morning circle, free play, snack, outside time, and story time. A week is seven bedtimes and seven breakfasts. Five minutes is when Daddy finishes brushing his teeth. Adults take for granted the information that young children still need to learn. You know without thinking that a bath takes longer than feeding the fish. You know it takes longer to finish that project at work if you stop for phone calls and email. But your child is not so skilled at eliminating distractions while cleaning up his toys. Entitlement-free parents teach the secret steps behind successful action.

Play

Entitlement-free children learn the value of effort and delayed gratification through being playfully engaged in the "work" of childhood: play. It's impossible to teach the abstract concept of entitlement-free thinking to a young child, but you can help him or her understand the importance of hard work through play. Play is active, hands-on, meaningful problem solving that sets the foundation for learning and for self-management. Through play, your child discovers something new every time, as each new experience becomes integrated into everything else he knew before this moment. Your child learns about getting things right and getting things wrong and about the satisfaction of time well spent. Entitlement-free behavior has to be translated into kid-speak, the language of play. Otherwise, entitlement-free living is only words, and important values need far more than lip service. Here are a few examples of important entitlement-free skills embedded in age-appropriate games and activities:

- Learning to play a board game teaches your child to take turns, to wait to move to prized spaces, and that someone will finish second.
- Playing with dolls or action figures gives your child an outlet for social drama: acting bossy, acting aggressive, or acting like a baby.
- Mastering a challenging jungle gym teaches your child to keep trying and that muscles get stronger.
- Making mud pies might be the perfect place to learn stress management.

- Seeing men-in-the-moon or stories-in-stars shows your child how to find a new way to solve an old problem.
- Negotiating positions in a game helps your child recognize other people's perspectives and his strengths relative to other people's needs.
- Fighting over the rules in a game of backyard soccer helps your child to understand which rules matter and which ones don't.

The list is endless as you imagine what's behind the decisions and actions involved in every form of play. The child without the time or space to engage in meaningful play never learns constructive alternatives to tantrums, to frustration, or to failure. Play is serious business, important and necessary. Play resizes adult situations to fit your child's particular age and ability.

Play is not passive entertainment. You know the difference by what your child adds to the experience. If your child watches a show or a video and is singing, dancing, and talking back to his newfound best friends, that's play. That's the meaningful engagement that gives your child practice with entitlement-free behavior and an outlet for entitlement behavior that is inappropriate in a non-play setting. These stories and songs become part of your child's emotional development—the story of Cinderella shows your child *how* to manage feeling sorry for herself when she gets stuck doing *all* the chores, and singing "We're the Pirates Who Don't Do Anything" with *Veggie Tales* allows your child to stomp his feet and protest, then get on with those non-optional jobs. If your child finishes watching one program and mindlessly looks for the next, you know he's trapped in a media-induced stupor. He needs an adult intervention.

It's easy to become dependent on entertainment as a quick fix. Those DVD players in cars will distract your child into complacency. But they can't teach your child to amuse himself, to engage other people, or to fill time creatively. The entitlement-free child is adaptable. He has inner resources to combat boredom and impatience.

Humor and Optimism

Laughter is essential to raising an entitlement-free child. It's good for the body, brain, and soul, and it promotes resilience and optimism, building strong families that know how to work and play together. It also creates connections between people despite differences and disagreements.

Humor is one of your best tools to fighting entitlement thinking. Find your child's humor buttons, whether it's pratfalls, limericks, or pure silliness, and use these to help ease emotional struggle and lift your child out of the solitary bubble of Me-Mine-Now. You can also use humor to divert a tantrum or defuse frustration:

- Act as if your feet are glued to the floor, or pretend the grocery cart is driving you. Surprise your children by letting them see you doing something unexpected.
- Let your child push the limits of appropriateness by reading silly books, like *Walter the Farting Dog* or *Good Families Don't*. Your child needs an outlet for silliness—farts and boogers included.
- Make up funny verses to *Down by the Bay* when you need to fill time. No props are required, only words.
- Be illogical. It may be animals that talk or cars that fly. With originality like that, your child just might become another Einstein or Bill Gates.

The ability to laugh actually stems from the entitlement-free ability to see a situation from another person's perspective. Three-year-olds can drive you crazy with their newly acquired ability to "get you" with a good joke. They will make you scream with a fake snake or roll on the floor laughing at the thought of Daddy wearing Mommy's bathing suit to work. Humor requires social skills as well as cognitive flexibility, and it opens the door to creative problem solving that helps your child to get unstuck in the sticky spots of day-to-day life. It fosters a forward-looking attitude that prepares your child to look past momentary struggles and see other possibilities. The entitlement-free child doesn't believe that "no" is the end of the world or that putting someone else first makes him last.

Age-Appropriate Expectations

The entitlement-free child knows what is expected and has the ability to meet those expectations. Expectations are age-appropriate when accompanied by love and guidance. Expectations that are too few, or too easy, fail to lead a child to his fullest potential. Expectations that are excessive, or are not accompanied with the tools to succeed, immobilize a child's progress. When you expect something difficult or challenging from your child, your child reacts the way you might react going to the dentist. If the dentist rushes you into the office without any comforting small talk and there's a thug standing beside your chair so you don't move, you will either comply but fear your next appointment or you will run for the hills. If the dentist tells you to come in for that root canal when you're in the mood, you might find a lot of better things to do until the problem is unavoidable and requires more intense treatment. If your dentist plays soothing music, tells you what he's doing next, and gives you breaks to rest your jaw, you might actually continue your annual appointments and floss regularly.

Age-appropriate expectations add clarity to a child's world. They communicate to a child an "I know you can" message. The best expectations provide a crystal ball to a future your child cannot see, like the dentist who knows a little discomfort today prevents major work next year. Your child doesn't know what he will know next year—you do. Your child doesn't know why some things feel so hard at times—you do. If your child picks up his toys today, it helps him find his toys tomorrow. If he learns to sit patiently on an airplane, he'll be able to visit grandparents more often. The entitlement-free parent accepts responsibility to be a loving teacher, not because "I said so" but because she understands the benefits to be gained. It's like keeping your teeth strong and healthy by going to the dentist.

Expectations change as your child grows and as situations change. Entitlement-free parents recognize the process of finding the "just right" expectation to fit the situation. Last month's expectations are not enough, while next year's are too much. To make it even more confusing, the expectation might fit the child but not the situation. For example, an expectation to pick up the toys needs modification if your child has a broken leg.

Entitlement-free expectations work because they balance these love and guidance considerations:

- **What and when:** Say what you want clearly and directly. "I want you to pick up the toys before dinner." Children aren't great mind readers, so their idea of "clean your room" may not resemble your idea.
- **How 1:** If you want it done a certain way, say it. "The books go on the bookcase, not in the toy bin."

Carefully evaluate your standards for reasonableness, and don't let perfectionism define success. Try to accept another "good way" besides your own.

- **How 2:** Anticipate and address potential snags. Be prepared to redirect if your child always gets distracted halfway through. For example, have him pass you the trucks before he tries to sit down and play with them. Or play Beat the Clock to keep him focused on the task at hand.

- **Why:** Add benefits to your acknowledgments. "Thanks! Now your room is organized for tomorrow's play date." Or, "You're getting faster and faster at finding all the puzzle pieces. I'll bet it feels good to be done quickly."

All learning requires a leap—from what is familiar to what is new. Your child willingly takes a risk when he sees certainty in your eyes, just as he holds back when he sees fear and doubt. Is the top of the slide safe, or is it too high? Is going on stage exciting or nerve-racking? Giving your child age-appropriate expectations honors his individuality and growth. Your child might need you to point the way, to hold his hand, and once in a while to give a gentle push. Each time, you earn your child's trust that your expectation is what's best for your child. That can feel like an enormous responsibility. Rest assured that it's okay to revise your expectations, particularly those that aren't working.

Expectations open the door to your child's potential. Like the compassionate dentist, it's up to you to lead your child through any challenging moment by finding the right balance between avoidance and frustration. The entitlement child and the fearful child never discover all that they *can* do. The entitlement-free child takes a chance and exceeds all expectations.

Security

When your child can anticipate what's coming next, he feels safe. He acquires age-appropriate power from a sense of control: "I know what's expected of me." Bedtime comes at a certain time. Dirty clothes go in the laundry basket. Book bags get emptied every night. Each expectation teaches your child to keep the chaos of daily life in check.

Predictable boundaries steer children toward good choices and responsibility. Every good choice reinforces the next good choice; asking for help feels better and is more effective than collapsing into a tantrum, and learning to wait for a turn makes a game more fun and last longer. Initially, loving adults make good choices on children's behalf: bedtimes, healthy food selections, safe toys. Then children gain control over themselves and their environment slowly and incrementally.

Children need a guidance system, just like bumper bowling. The bumpers keep the ball in play by eliminating gutter balls until the bowler has sufficient skill to bowl without them. Age-appropriate expectations guide your child's choices to avoid a free-for-all. Otherwise, continually repeating poor choices undermines future decision-making ability and entitlement-free responsibility. For example, children can't choose healthy foods from a fast-food diet, and children can't choose to clean up litter at the park if they're playing computer games all day. Eventually, there comes a time when the bowler is old enough and strong enough to throw the ball without bumpers, even if the bowler doesn't have the skill. Gutter balls and mistakes are expected after a certain age, without taking the fun out of the game.

Rules of the Game

Rules define the game, just as they tell the bowlers where to throw the ball after the bumper guards are removed. Rules are the roadmap to entitlement-free behavior. When you see your child or your family moving off course, as you'll see in many of the situations in Chapters 4 through 10, find the most direct way to bring them back. When you find yourself nagging or bickering over the same thing day after day, it's time for a new rule. Communicate clearly and concisely what it is that will make things go more smoothly. Rules alleviate the strain of explaining and negotiating the same thing over and over again.

The best rules reflect the mutual respect and personal responsibility of entitlement-free behavior. But there aren't any particular rules for all families to follow. In one house, phones and televisions must be off at dinnertime. In another house, thank-you notes must be written before you can play with gifts. Rules are effective when they clarify "how to do things better." Rules create habits for living well in your family and in your community. Keep 'em simple:

- **Choose wisely.** One well-chosen rule is better than a long list of wishful thinking. Be realistic about the number of rules. If your spouse can't remember them, your child probably can't either.
- **Stick to it.** All rules must be enforceable; otherwise the rules will not be taken seriously. The criterion of enforceability is not whether you can "make" your child comply, but whether you are willing to invest the time and effort. If your rule is to do homework before dinner, you have to make it a family priority: You might have to cancel other plans or be prepared

to delay dinner a few nights until the rule becomes the habit.

Rules, like other expectations, make life together easier. They soften out the conflicts of living and learning. The entitlement-free child respects rules because he lives in a world where rules are taken seriously by the adults who stand behind them. He reaps the benefits of rules by learning how to live with others less stressfully.

Living with No

Saying no to your child when appropriate is the entitlement-free prerogative to make a good choice on behalf of your child. The entitlement-free child may not always like hearing no, but it isn't the end of the world. Positive rules help to avoid power struggles and help guide children to good choices. Sometimes, particularly in safety situations, no is no, while other times, a creative yes is still a no.

Before they have the maturity to evaluate all the aspects of a situation, children need to learn to live by established limits. Limits teach children restraint when they want to lash out in anger or frustration, and they help them learn how much is enough. Without limits, a child may hurt other people or engage in destructive actions. Limits create a safety cushion around your child until the time when he can make better choices.

The entitlement-free parent becomes skilled at setting limits through practice and trial and error. The first time you plan an afternoon with friends at the park, you don't realize your child will be cranky at 6:30 p.m.—too late for a nap and too early for bed. The next time, you'll know; regardless of his protests, you'll be the first ones to leave. Trial and error also teaches you to say no to really fun sleepovers when your child isn't feeling 100 percent, or that he's really just stalling when he asks for "one more story" at night. Entitlement-free parents know how to say "no" when it's important without creating a legacy of "can't do." Choosing your battles means overlooking the superhero cape every day after school and the bathtub overcrowded with toys.

It takes conviction to say no like you mean it. Entitlement-free parents stand their ground when they are being tested, and they strive for consistency under pressure. Saying "maybe" or "ask me tomorrow" strings your child along with false hope. So how should you respond to "But whyyyyyyyy?" Entitlement-free parents know better than to get sucked into that no-win situation. They might lob the question right back to the child—"Hmmm, why do *you* think it's a good idea to eat dinner at the table with the rest of us?" Or they rephrase the old "because I said so" into "it's my job to… (pick one) teach you right from wrong, keep you safe, or make a grown-up choice."

Entitlement-free parents also know when to present options and when options are not available. Generally speaking, it's okay to give your child a choice except when one choice turns into ten. Then he's just pushing your buttons. You might also turn a no into a yes without compromising the ultimate outcome—yes, you can invite your friends over tomorrow (instead of today) and yes, you can brush your teeth before picking up your toys (as long as you don't forget).

Being a "no-sayer" or the enforcer of rules is not always comfortable when you'd rather be the "fun parent." But the good-cop/bad-cop routine doesn't work in entitlement-free households, because every smart child knows how to work one against the other and pave a new path to entitlement indulgences. In the end, the "no-sayers" are parents the entitlement-free child can trust to make good decisions.

THE ENTITLEMENT-FREE ADVANTAGE

Entitlement-free children are happier than entitlement children, because they understand themselves and the world in good times and in difficult times. They have confidence, not because they are perfect in a perfect world, but because they know their strengths and can adapt to a variety of people and situations. They also have the emotional resilience it takes to bounce back from temporary setbacks, whether it's a low grade or a missed party invitation. Entitlement-free children are better equipped to handle those bullies on the playground and the queen-bee cliques in the school cafeteria when they are older, because they have not been sheltered from negative situations. Entitlement-free children take responsibility to rally inner and outer resources to succeed. They've learned that success is not automatic. It's created by words and actions over time.

Entitlement-free children look for ways to help others, and they trust that others will help them. By creating a sense of connection and mutual responsibility in early childhood, the entitlement-free child is the first to volunteer to respond to people in need—they send toys to hurricane children and take balloons to the children's hospitals. They organize a Paperclip Project to build a Holocaust monument and Pennies for Peace to educate children in Central Asia. Entitlement-free children know that everyone is not the same—people do not feel the same, think the same, or act the same—but everyone shares a common humanity.

Becoming an entitlement-free family is a positive change for families with too much—too much stress, too much guilt, and too much to do. But entitlement-free living is also a positive change for families with *not* enough—not enough time, not enough energy, and not enough sanity. The entitlement-free family steps off the entitlement hamster wheel; they're done running fast and getting nowhere. Entitlement is insatiable. The entitlement-free family has something more worthwhile to do. Since they aren't trying to have it all, they really can live today. They are able to turn off the cell phones for twenty minutes at dinner. They can pick the kindergarten based on where their child will thrive instead of being sold on the fast-track for Ivy League hopefuls.

Your child is capable. You can lead your child into a future rich with his or her fullest potential. It's never too late to start making entitlement-free changes. The next chapter will help you recognize the ways others succumb to the entitlement myth, and it will give you a bird's-eye view of entitlement-free choices in everyday family situations. Then you will have the entitlement-free resources to join together to build a new entitlement-free community.

3

ENTITLEMENT-FREE PARENTING

So, how do we get back to the good ol' days of respect and integrity? A simple click of the heels won't transport you back to entitlement-free living. The answer isn't in the pre-entitlement parenting of the fifties and sixties. Those authoritarian models of parenting didn't work, and we're long past the notion that children should be seen and not heard. Populations and opportunities have grown, and global connections are instantaneous. The new world of technology can't be erased, nor should it be. Children are plugged in and thumb-savvy. Today's toys are here to stay. Entitlement-free parenting begins in this world and defines a new future that borrows the best of everything we now know.

We know plenty from research and from common sense:

- **Entitlement-free parents must meet the essential needs of children as they grow and change.** Sure, entitlement-free parents love and protect, feed and clothe, and educate; but then what? After that, the details start to get a little confusing. Is ice cream essential? What about a bedtime story? What if you're stalking your child's coach at the grocery store to plead for a schedule change? Entitlement-free parenting requires ongoing decisions about what's right and wrong, what works and doesn't work. But that's so much better than measuring your child against the entitlement checklist: pretty clothes—check; good neighborhood—check; enrichment programs—check, check.

- **Entitlement-free parents must balance age-appropriate expectations with supportive nurturing.** It's that love and guidance combo. But how do you really know when you're tipping the scales too far in one direction? Entitlement-free parenting gives you the ability to recognize the warning signs when you start down the entitlement slide. You will have the entitlement-free power, wisdom, and authority to self-correct.

- **Entitlement-free thinking must acknowledge the needs of parents in a well-functioning family.** Happy parents are less stressed. They listen when the flight attendants tell them to put on their oxygen mask first. But what can you do on the day that your work schedule is in conflict with the school play, when you have to send your child to school with the green stuff dripping from her nose, when you'd lay down your life for your child but you want to cry because your needs are last on the list, after the dog's and gerbil's? Entitlement-free parenting says it's not an either/or, kids or parents proposition. Every entitlement-free choice moves your family closer to a family life you can actually live with.

  Entitlement-free thinking defines a new family in an ever-changing world. Entitlement-free parenting is a decision-making strategy based on mutual and self-respect. But it begins with some very definite assumptions about your role as a parent and about your child at different stages of development. Because, after all, it's not only about your child. These assumptions are the building blocks for living together as a family and living well in a community.

CORE ASSUMPTIONS FOR ENTITLEMENT-FREE PARENTING

1. You cannot "make" your child happy all the time.

2. You are absolutely, unequivocally, irrefutably smarter than your child.

3. You are the grown-up, not your child's friend.

4. Your child should have age-appropriate power.

5. Your child is not you.

6. Your child lives in a diverse world.

7. Your child prepares today for the unexpected tomorrow.

You Cannot "Make" Your Child Happy All the Time

Of course she deserves to be happy, but happy is not a permanent state. So it's unrealistic to believe you can always make your child happy. One emotion cannot sustain your child in all of life's various situations. You don't want your child to be happy when she sees her friend trip and fall, or to pretend to be happy when she's hurt or sad.

You *do* want your child to feel safe and secure in any situation. Your child needs to know that non-happy emotions aren't scary things, whether they are her own emotions or the emotions of other people. Imagine, instead of having to spin your child in a protective cocoon of perfect "happiness," you can give your child a life jacket that will keep her afloat in sunshine and in storms, for the rest of her life. The entitlement-free child learns to recognize and express the full range of human emotions: happiness, sadness, anger, frustration, confusion, curiosity, and more. Even very young children can learn to feel secure in themselves, with guidance from loving adults.

Learn to recognize the emotional life of your child. From infancy to adulthood, your child's emotional life grows and changes. Babies learn they are loved and lovable by learning to trust and enjoy the world. They are able to conquer frustration by learning to crawl, walk, and speak. They also learn through patience that people will come through for them tomorrow, or a week later. Mommy and Daddy still love them after new babies arrive at home or at the end of a very difficult day.

A young child learns emotional stability through ordinary daily challenges. She learns that things get better—boo-boos heal, and so do hurt feelings. People make mistakes and then make them right. In Chapter 5, you will learn how to teach your child to master challenging emotions.

You Are Absolutely, Unequivocally, Irrefutably Smarter than Your Child

In order to be effective as your child's teacher and guide, you must be able to handle anything your child throws at you— metaphorically, that is. You don't have to know everything, and you don't have to be perfect. You only need to use what you already know and remember. Experience is on your side.

Each stage in your child's evolving development brings new surprises and uncertainties that create doubt and confusion to you as a parent. What worked so well yesterday may not work today, because your child grew—cognitively, emotionally, socially, or physically. What worked so well with one child is like speaking a foreign language to another child.

It's a gift of parenthood that until adolescence, your child, for the most part, believes that you know almost everything and you can fix just about anything. These beliefs are fundamentally woven into your child's heart. Take a deep breath and smile. Despite any evidence to the contrary, your child has elected you to parenthood. You will now spend the next few decades earning that privilege.

Nothing's perfect, though, and there will be cracks in the mirror. Parenthood will drive you bonkers. When you come face to face with your fallible and fragile human side, you will need adult support. Turn to your own parents, your spouse, or your friends for support, respite, or a fresh perspective. Laugh, scream, or bang your head against a soft wall. Just try to be a little mature about it—choose how and when you fall apart. It's better to ask adults to sustain adults-in-need than to ask the children. And even when you are completely lost chasing your child into uncharted developmental territory, you will always have the capacity to know more than your child.

You Are the Grown-Up, Not Your Child's Friend

You can be your child's partner, accomplice, confidant, and ally. But you need to be a grown-up too. By all means, have fun with your child. A home without joy is the saddest place of all. Laugh, sing, dance, and play. Children learn best and most when they are engaged in playful experiences. Routines and chores are fun. They are opportunities to be just like you—strong, smart, and capable.

Do not mistake your child for a grown-up in a little body. Your child lives in a magical place called childhood, where logic and reason have their own rules. Inanimate objects are alive, and people can appear or disappear without warning. Try to understand the world from your child's point of view, by being thoughtful, considerate, and age-appropriate without compromising your authority as a parent. Children are not safe without grown-up people guarding childhood. The entitlement-free parent protects the magical world of childhood with rules and routines: nutritious meals, restful sleep, regular baths, and trips to doctors. When parents act like a child's friend, they forfeit their grown-up power and allow the children to decide what's best. It becomes a challenge to do little things, like holding ice on a bump, and harder things, like enforcing curfews.

Your child has given you a gift—an invitation to come into her world. You can visit, but you have a job to do that's more than being a friend. You meet your child in that wonderful place of Santa Claus and fairy dust, story characters who are as real as friends, and kisses that can make everything better. Enjoy yourself. Treasure each and every visit, because they will pass all too quickly. But keep this in mind: you are there to welcome your child into your world too.

The most awesome magic happens when grown-ups create the bridge from one child's personal childhood sanctuary to that child's ownership of his piece of the real world. Your child may outgrow dragons and tooth fairies, but she never really leaves childhood behind. It fortifies her forever. Be your child's grown-up guide to all the new adventures awaiting her.

Your Child Should Have Age-Appropriate Power

Your child needs age-appropriate power to progress from dependence to independence. Entitlement-free parenting is not taking all the power from children. Instead, it's giving children the power they can manage at a given time, honoring their ever-growing abilities. As with politicians, an imbalance of power has an enormous potential to corrupt. Your role as a parent is to monitor your child's responsible use of power.

The taste of power is alluring, and children often overestimate how much they can handle. Children are also notorious for poor judgment. So you as a parent might feel like you are constantly engaged in negotiations. Which lessons should your child learn on his own, and when should you make the right choice for your child? You will find help in the chapters ahead as you claim your quiet power and test your child's resourcefulness.

Because your child grows through active participation with other people and the real world, she needs to learn how to make good decisions and to see the consequences of her actions. Brains as well as bodies grow through hands-on experimentation. Your child learns to use her power constructively when she is allowed to do things for herself: from pouring milk to climbing a jungle gym, from ordering in a restaurant to finding all the pieces to her favorite toy. She learns to use her power negatively when people will do anything to appease a temper tantrum or she's scaling tall bookcases, playing superhero.

The entitlement-free child is able to build her decision-making "muscles" over time. Gradually, the parent adds a little more power and a little more weight, and the muscles slowly grow. Along the way, the child may make a few bad decisions—but that's the only way to learn how to make good decisions. It's up to you to give your child the decision-making practice, and eventually, she will earn trust and independence.

Your Child Is Not You

From the time your child said her first no, she was establishing a sense of her own identity. You already know that your child was born with her own temperament, her own unique strengths, and her own interests and talents. To help your child reach her fullest potential, celebrate your child's strengths and teach your child how to compensate for her weaknesses. As a parent, you will undoubtedly come face to face with your own strengths and weaknesses as well, and it's natural to try to protect your child from difficulties you may have experienced. These past experiences automatically color your parenting, but ultimately your child is separate from you, with different strengths and weaknesses. There'll be times when you may have to ask yourself, "Is this about me or about my child?"—when you're pushing to get front-row seats to the Wiggles concert or when you're angry that the cool kids ignore her on the playground. Strive to recognize your child's personal strengths, to find value in challenges, and to appreciate what lies behind all success. Then your child will excel at the things that truly matter.

Will you be judged by your child's successes and failures? Sure you will, but you have the right to choose whose opinion you value. The gossips and the "I'll-never-do-that-when-I'm-a-parent" critics leverage your emotions. Focus on what's best for your child, not what other people think. Should your child be reading on par with her same-age cousin? Should she be watching less TV or more TV? Should she be allowed to eat sweets with her friends? Listen to their comments with an open mind, if you can. Ask for another perspective when you think you need one. Surround yourself with people you trust who share your values, and do the best you can to guide your child on her unique path.

Your Child Lives in a Diverse World

Family life and an ever-expanding social network of school, friends, and community open your child's heart and mind to the influences of other people. Simple tasks for adults, like sharing, listening, and waiting, are complex developmental skills for children. Your child begins to realize that some people look and act differently, and that other people have different needs and different expectations. Sometimes other children do things that your child doesn't like.

Your child's social skills begin at home with siblings and parents, even the dog. Basic principles of social interaction build upon one another as your child's social circles grow to include extended family members, neighbors, babysitters, teachers, and classmates—possibly to helping children on the other side of the planet. Entitlement children expect everyone to do things their way—"If Mommy lets me sit in her lap at the restaurant, you should too," or "If I can play outside without shoes in the backyard, why should I have to wear shoes at school?" Adaptability in these ordinary situations transfers into cultural adaptability later.

A primal parenting instinct is to find the one right way of doing something and getting everyone else on the same page. Mom might have felt this the first time Dad held the baby in a non-Mom way. But wise Mom eventually learned to bite her tongue, knowing that Dad's nontraditional style was perfectly harmless. The lifelong parenting challenge is to cultivate your positive influence while preparing your child to maneuver in a diverse world. In the entitlement-free world, schools have the right to ask you to arrive earlier than you like, store clerks may ask your child to walk in the aisles, and you never throw your litter out the car window just because you're tired of holding it.

What works in one home may not work in another. The rules at grandparents' homes may be different than at your child's home. Classrooms reflect the individual personalities of teachers, and different sports emphasize different mental dispositions. Childhood is a time of guided experimentation, acquiring new skills, and applying them to new situations. As an entitlement-free parent, you may know what's best for your child, but you still need to make concessions to the wishes of other people, particularly when you are in their homes and businesses.

Your Child Prepares Today for the Unexpected Tomorrow

Making peanut butter and jelly sandwiches in 2009 might be one of a thousand experiences that leads your child to the greatest scientific discovery of 2040. You can only imagine what your child's future will hold. The ability to solve problems is an essential skill that is developed in childhood. Every age and stage in development presents your child with ordinary challenges to ensure that she learns what she needs to know.

Childhood garbage collectors grow up to be innovative CEOs, and cape-wearing superheroes grow up to be pediatricians. Meaningful engagement in childhood brings heart, mind, and body together. The combination ignites a fire around your child's potential as she internalizes a lifelong attitude about living and learning.

Life skills are accumulated from a hodgepodge of places: at kitchen counters, in bathtubs, and in wide open spaces.

The entitlement-free parent stokes the fire by encouraging daily, personal problem solving. Then your child is ready for success and for any challenges that pop up to surprise her along the way. The entitlement child recognizes opportunities, gathers helpful resources, and steers around potential obstacles. An entitlement-free child "owns" the world, not out of fear or envy, but with a sense of responsibility to make it happen.

ENTITLEMENT-FREE PARENTING ISN'T DIFFICULT

As a matter of fact, it probably reflects your parenting goals far better than other strategies. The problem with parenting isn't good advice versus bad advice, but sorting out the confusing messages. With parenting sound bites constantly on the news and "experts" everywhere, it's tempting to look for the Cliff's Notes. Parenting advice you hear in the media may be true enough, but trying to apply the suggestions to your family on any given day is never as easy as it sounds, especially in desperate parenting moments. For example, if you just had an exhausting day at work and your child asks oh-so-sweetly for an extra hour of computer time, you might think, "Why not? I can use the break." Besides, she deserves a break after all that homework, doesn't she? You hear all the time about this generation of stressed-out kids.

What's wrong with this picture? That easy-looking, sound-bite solution is going to make your life twice as hard. It's okay to be flexible with rules, but it's not okay to be arbitrary. Giving in here is a quick fix for tonight, but the problem won't go away. What will you say when your child asks the same question tomorrow and the day after? The better answer, the one that truly will give you peace of mind, is the one that addresses the genuine problem. In this case, it starts with taking care of parent stress, because your child absorbs your stress far faster than stress from the outside world. There's no shame in feeling tired or less than perfect, but you can still show your child constructive ways to alleviate stress or manage difficult days without breaking your own rules. In all honesty, you're probably not choosing computer time as a remedy for school stress; it's just a temporary distraction.

Entitlement-free choices lead you to parenting in the big picture. It is the easiest way to finally stop problems from spiraling out of control, as opposed to entitlement responses that tease you with quick fixes.

STAY ON COURSE

Parenting is like driving a car (sometimes a Formula One race car!). It's best to learn what you need to know in advance, before you have to make a split-second decision in traffic. A clever driver can avoid crashing into the wall on most days. An experienced driver stays on course because she knows the car and the track under all sorts of conditions, she can antici-pate the other drivers' driving styles, and she knows her own limits from past mistakes. She drives around the obstacles when someone else is spinning out of control.

In most day-to-day parenting, you can shoot from the hip and hope for the best. Quick fixes get you through the day, when you don't have time to deliberate the pros and cons of every parenting choice. Your cleverness will guide you, your child will be safe, and you absolutely don't need to worry that you're setting your child on a path of doom. You can think on your feet under less-than-ideal conditions like sleep deprivation or nail-biting fear. In other times of stress, however, certain inexperienced reactions lead to disastrous results. Quick fixes that never work, or never work for very long, include:

- **Hysterical or desperate behavior.** Parenting is emotional, as it should be, because your job is to raise little people who think and feel. But your child cannot hear your message when your emotions are spilling out of control.
- **Threats and bribes.** Behind every threat or bribe is a sense of powerlessness that undermines the value of what you're trying to teach. Find a strong place to stand before trying to support someone else.
- **Appeasement.** Giving in buys you only temporary peace of mind. You are setting yourself up for a shakedown next time, and the time after that.
- **Avoidance.** Sweeping things under the rug makes for a very bumpy rug. Pretending a problematic situation will improve by itself is not realistic. Take some time to think about it first.

Entitlement-free parenting alerts you to these red flags immediately. There'll still be days when you wish you had a magic wand to make yourself or your child disappear. And entitlement-free parenting says to take the break you deserve. Just don't make choices that undermine what you're trying to teach.

There are many ways to stay on course as an entitlement-free parent. You can prepare in advance for ongoing discipline struggles instead of blindly reacting. You can monitor your stress, anxiety, and frustration. You can create routines and schedules that work for your family. In the end, you can confidently make parenting choices today that meet your child's needs today and tomorrow.

ONE-SIZE PARENTING DOESN'T FIT ALL

Your day-to-day parenting choices will not be identical to someone else's choices. While parents of entitlement-free children share basic assumptions, each parent has to customize what works to fit each individual child and what makes sense in your home. Your home is a reflection of you—your strengths, your personality, your quirkiness.

There is no substitute for you. There is no perfect team who would do and say all the right things better than you—not a baby nurse, sleep consultant, nutritionist, teacher, tutor, or behavior specialist. The experts are here to serve you, not replace you. Emotional attachment and cognitive learning are interconnected. Your child grows best in a home where she is nurtured by people who uniquely love her. The objective, well-trained observer can give you a fresh perspective, but the right answer without a personal connection is hollow and shallow.

If a parenting strategy is working, use it regardless of all expert opinions to the contrary. Don't fix what isn't broken. Ignore the advice for now. If something truly is wrong for your family, you will get other unmistakable signals that it's time for a change. The misbehavior will escalate until it cannot be ignored any longer. Focus on today. You have plenty of time to deal with future problems in the future.

Once in a while, you may feel like you are alone on an island and everyone else is at a party on a cruise ship. It happens. You know that teatime at the Ritz-Carlton instead of an overdue nap spells D-I-S-A-S-T-E-R and that twenty dollars' worth of tokens at an indoor game-room throws your child into game-aholic frenzy. A good parent, at one time or another, stands alone. People might criticize you. They might chastise you into doing things their way. Consider their opinions, if it's worthwhile. This is surely a prime opportunity to be a problem-solving role model for your child.

PRACTICE, PRACTICE, PRACTICE

Parenting is practice. Experience is a great teacher, because in each new situation, you learn something new about yourself and your child. You learn what pushes your buttons, what causes you stress, when your child falls apart, and how your child rebounds from difficulties. You develop a style and a swagger that says you are ready for anything, because experience loads you up with a bag full of useful parenting tricks:

- to make boredom interesting (the ultimate gift of time)
- to use games and routines instead of demands and ultimatums
- to say no with confidence
- to create connections to others
- to turn mistakes into opportunities

Entitlement-free parents know how to observe and adapt, laugh and grow. Entitlement-free parents also know from experience that sometimes they sabotage their own efforts and sometimes other sabotaging influences temporarily throw them off course. It takes patience to deconstruct the myths of false entitlement.

As you read descriptions of real-life parenting situations in the chapters ahead, you will acquire skills from other people's experience. You will recognize the slippery slope when you say, "What's the harm if...?" and find yourself buried in an avalanche of false compromises. You will not fall for "all or nothing," and you'll discover the freedom of "the third way." You'll reframe false intuitions like "she can't do that" or "she needs me" (of course she needs you—just not exactly the way you imagine). And you won't be held hostage to contradictory beliefs, as in "she's bored—she's a genius."

Learn how to be entitlement-free anywhere, anytime—at home, with friends, at school, in public places. The choice is yours, and it's much easier than you think.

PART II

Entitlement-Free Strategies for Everyday Situations

The upcoming chapters address the various situations at home, in school, and around the neighborhood that shape entitlement or entitlement-free attitudes. You do not have to follow the suggestions verbatim. Instead, adapt them to your personal style and to the needs of your individual child. The examples may go into more detail than is suitable for your needs. Your personal situations may warrant less action or less talking.

A primary challenge of entitlement-free parenting is deciding when to actively intervene and when to let children work things out independently. Generally speaking, if a situation is self-correcting, don't get involved. This is true for minor playground disputes as well as tantrums and whining. On the other hand, you want to step in if the behavior is setting a new precedent that will have to be "un-taught" tomorrow. Children learn what they do; hitting grown-ups, running around restaurants, or ignoring you are things that are guaranteed to be repeated if permitted.

Another rule of thumb for entitlement-free parenting is this: Talk less in discipline moments. Explanations for young children usually can be wrapped up in one or two sentences. Short and sweet gives you maximum clarity. Use those same few sentences repeatedly to remind your child and guide him through sticky situations. Feel free to engage your child in rich language experiences, even discussions about the problem behavior, as you go about your natural day—just not while you're trying to set or enforce limits.

Entitlement-free parenting balances intervention and independence. Sometimes it's the invisible hand that supports independence, like coaching your child to take back his toy from his intimidating sister. Other times, a situation escalates without decisive parent involvement, as when the same intimidating sister locks him out of the house.

Entitlement-free parenting requires perspective. It is an ongoing process. Try to be patient in your own situations, as they often reveal surprising connections and original solutions.

4

HOME

- **Make room for kid-time and independence in the family's daily schedule.**
- **Give your child concrete ways to help at home.**
- **Expect to be tested, even when you do everything "right."**

Home is your child's first context for living with others. A child's family is both an extension of who he is and his first encounter with people who think and feel differently than he does. The entitlement-free child knows he is part of a unique and wonderful family who care about each other and care for each other, today and always. Routines, respect, and responsibility that begin at home are key ingredients to raising an entitlement-free child. Most conflicts in the home overlook some aspect of one or more of these three ingredients to a successful family life.

Routines
Routines help steer your child away from "I want it now" thinking, creating predictable order for daily life. They teach

the entitlement-free child how to use time effectively and to trust that there's enough time after "now." They are your best tool in fighting the time battles—trying to do anything within a limited amount of time. Children notoriously take longer to do things and get sidetracked more often. Routines ensure that what needs to happen in a day does, and they guarantee time together with your child despite busy schedules.

Respect

Respect is that deep regard for your own well-being as well as the interests of others. Self-respect and mutual respect go hand in hand. The entitlement-free child is respected by his family; he is seen and heard. He has respect for himself as capable and resourceful, helpful not helpless. He gives respect to others, because he assumes value in another's point of view.

Responsibility

Responsibility gives the entitlement-free child the opportunity to be competent in a family. Families love, work, and play together. Play is not merely leisure—it's the laughter and the fun of being in this together. In an entitlement-free family, "work" is not a bad word. Families take care of one another—eating, sleeping, washing, sharing time and space. The entitlement-free child thrives as an active participant in the stuff of living together, contributing in meaningful, age-appropriate ways.

Entitlement-free parenting makes living in real families possible again. Living with children is exhausting. You try really hard, and then you have to do it all again tomorrow. As you will see in the following situations, entitlement-free homes are not perfect. They are definitely not conflict-free. But each conflict leads to a realistic solution for real-life families, helping to build an entitlement-free home environment. The promise of entitlement-free parenting is that there is joy to be found in being together as a family—more joy than in anything you can buy.

MORNING CHAOS

Situation: My child *won't* cooperate when we have to get out of the house on weekday mornings. It's one fight after another, and I feel so bad dropping him off at school after a stressful morning.

Entitlement Issues: You want to respect your child's independence and autonomy. Unfortunately, the entitlement child learns that he gets what he wants, whether or not it's good for him. The child is the one in charge, but in this case he is not capable of making good decisions. The entitlement child also discovers that smart adults will defer to him in order to avoid feeling bad themselves.

Entitlement-Free Perspective: Mornings are difficult for many reasons—poor planning, not enough sleep, too many distractions, and serious time constraints. Everyone runs out of time eventually. Blaming a child is absolutely counterproductive. Your child wants the same kind of morning you do. He needs to see you make good decisions before he can.

The entitlement-free child is both capable and respectful. Give your child an active role in problem solving while establishing clear boundaries to maximize success. The entitlement-free child will be proud of what he can do instead of being empowered by negativity.

ENTITLEMENT-FREE STRATEGIES

1. **Reclaim your confidence.** You can't change anything if you question your ability. Avoid screaming and emotional drama. Do as much as you can in advance to control your stress. The night before, make sure your child's school uniform is washed and the car keys are where they should be.

2. **Talk to your child the night before.** Explain in one or two sentences that mornings are not working the way they are right now and you're looking forward to a better way, in which there'll be less fighting.

3. **Identify where you need to make concrete changes.** Do you need to wake up your child earlier? Set a limit on certain activities? You may want to designate fifteen minutes for breakfast, ten minutes to get dressed, or the maximum number of snooze buttons. Do you need to get yourself dressed earlier so you are able to help your child? Make concrete changes that your child can understand: set a game timer and play Beat the Clock. Get better organized: store backpacks and shoes near the door or pack lunches with your child the night before.

4. **Communicate the plan to your child.** You can't succeed alone, so be sure your child knows what's expected of him. Make it short and sweet: "Tomorrow we start our new no-fighting mornings." Or: "Tomorrow we make it to the car with all our stuff by 7:30."

5. **Anticipate what could go wrong.** If your child reenacts Moses parting the Red Sea in his bowl of oatmeal every day, you might need to set a specific time to have the dishes in the sink. Or remember to check to see if your

child sat down to watch TV again or is making soap castles in the bathroom sink. Be proactive to get your child back on track.

6. **Keep moving forward, calmly and confidently, no matter what.** Stick to the priorities. If you're fighting over socks, forget the socks but get the shoes. When it's time to go, just go. You can finesse the details tomorrow.

STUBBORNNESS

Situation: My child absolutely refuses to get in the car when it's time to leave. She sits down defiantly and crosses her arms as if to say, "Make me."

Entitlement Issues: Your child was born tenacious, and you don't want to change her. She's entitled to be her true self. Besides, why not choose your battles? It's much easier just to call work and tell them you'll be a few minutes late. Or consider these other entitlement rationalizations: "I'm my own boss, so I can be late" and "My family is more important than work, so I should take time when my child is having a hard time." Both statements are true but miss the entitlement repercussions.

Entitlement-Free Perspective: It's not okay for children to deliberately make parents late for work or to be late for school when it's avoidable. Your child suffers when she's given negative power over you. Entitlement-free parents stay out of the power struggle while maintaining focus on the goal. Should you "choose your battle," you don't want it to be in response to deliberate defiance.

Do not beg, bribe, or lecture in the heat of the moment. The entitlement-free child learns as much from *how* you teach as from *what* you teach. Discuss the situation later, in the car after school or at the end of the day when you talk about your day. Say, "Remember when you sat down and didn't want to get in the car this morning? That was really hard. Let's find another way to help you get to school on time." The entitlement-free child learns that cooperation works better than defiance.

ENTITLEMENT-FREE STRATEGIES

1. **Expect defiance if your child is in one of those oppositional stages that occurs with every growth spurt.** Give yourself additional time during these stages, and start going to the car fifteen minutes early. (In the best-case scenario, you'll have time for a Starbucks after you drop off your child at school early.) Distract your child before the sit-in with an "important task," like using the Dustbuster to vacuum the car seats. (Everyone wins!)

2. **Don't fall for the power play.** Ignore the behavior but not your child. Quietly walk up to your child and whisper that it's time to go. Take her hand and go.

3. **Use humor.** Your child has backed herself into a corner that she doesn't know how to get out of with dignity. Humor sends your child a lifeline and gives her a way to get out gracefully. Say, "I want to tell my daughter that it's time to go, but I think she's turned into a rock and can't hear me. Oh, Daughter, can you hear me? It's time to go. I think I'll go to the car and wait for my rock to roll out the door."

4. **Don't give up.** Undesirable behavior may escalate. Your child is testing you to see if you really mean what you

say. Inconsistency now teaches your child to push a little harder or a little longer for the rules to change.

SHORT-ORDER COOK

Situation: Everyone wants something different for dinner. I feel like a short-order cook working twice as hard trying to make everyone happy.

Entitlement Issues: The entitlement child learns to take without regard for the person who's giving. You want to please everyone, but you are exhausted jumping through hoops. The entitlement child also misses the opportunity to change his opinion of things because the world is "made to order" to fit his needs. He doesn't get a chance to revise his likes and dislikes over time. He doesn't have to adapt to the world; the world adapts to him.

Entitlement-Free Perspective: It's not your job to entice your child to eat. It's your job to offer healthy food without the emotional melodrama. The entitlement-free child is responsible for choosing to eat or not eat what's offered. He learns to make good choices over time. The entitlement-free child is taught the value of appreciation and gratitude through ongoing mealtime routines and rituals. He learns to contribute to mealtime routines rather than merely complain.

ENTITLEMENT-FREE STRATEGIES

1. **Set ground rules that work in your home.** Should everyone eat the same thing? Do you want to offer a no-cook option, like peanut butter and jelly? Keep it simple and consistent. Your child's search for the perfect

food is driven more often by the enticement of pushing your buttons than by an actual appetite.

2. **Communicate the new expectations to your child.** "From now on, we're serving one meal, and you can decide to eat the portions you like." Or, "If you don't like what we're having for dinner, let me know *before* you come to the table."

3. **Clarify after-dinner rules.** You don't want to revert to the short-order cook routine an hour later. Decide in advance what the nighttime eating rules will be: you might leave something on the refrigerator shelf that your child can get for himself; or you might explain that the kitchen closes at 8:00 p.m. and he'll need to wait for breakfast. (He'll live…really.)

4. **Teach gratitude and table manners.** There will be times when your child doesn't like some foods, so talk about how to say, "No, thank you." Also practice how to express compliments and appreciation. The best compliments are the most original. Let your child finish the sentence: "This pasta's better than a restaurant meal because…" or "I wonder if the cook was thinking about [this] when he was cooking tonight." Mealtimes are not only times to eat; they are also times to be silly while teaching conversation skills.

5. **Get your child involved.** Your child can fix a salad, mix up a dip for veggies, or scramble eggs. Search for child-friendly preparations like quesadillas, kebabs, and chili. Hands-on helpers are proud chefs and more cooperative eaters.

6. **Write upcoming menu items on a kitchen black-board (or post pictures) to reinforce delayed gratification.** Your child may not like Dad's favorite dinner tonight, but tomorrow will be his favorite. By modeling respectful communication, you give your child an appropriate voice in family decision making.

BEDTIME OPPOSITION

Situation: My child fights us at bedtime, so she stays up with us until she falls asleep on the sofa.

Entitlement Issues: You can rationalize that children know whether they are tired or not, or that you can't force a child to sleep when her body isn't ready. Or that this extra snuggle time feels really sweet after a busy day. More often than not, the entitlement child is introducing chaos by undermining the parents' decision-making ability. Parents are giving in instead of planning ahead for nurturing time.

Entitlement-Free Perspective: Falling asleep in bed is a major step toward independence—your child is learning to feel safe when she can't immediately see the people she loves. The entitlement-free child learns to understand that sleep is good for growing a healthy body and mind. Devise your nighttime plan to respond to your child's needs while still giving her the tools to master the situation. The entitlement-free child learns to accept the end of another fun day and look forward to tomorrow. Exhausted parents earn a well-deserved break and some equally important adult time.

ENTITLEMENT-FREE STRATEGIES

1. **Plan "together time" earlier in the day, so you're not feeling guilty at bedtime.** Ten minutes of your undivided attention after breakfast or before dinner can do wonders at bedtime.

2. **Give your child the facts.** Bodies and brains need rest at night to help them grow. Active children try to function on less sleep so they don't miss any of the fun, but those aren't good decisions, because you need a good night's sleep to feel better the next day.

3. **Respect your child's ability to listen to her body, to know whether or not she's tired.** Your job isn't to force your child to sleep. It's to create an optimal bedtime routine for everyone in the house. Discuss all the things your child can do in her bed when she's not tired: read, tell finger stories (acting out the drama with talking, wiggling fingers), talk to the stuffed animal, look at the stars, or go to faraway places in her imagination.

4. **Give your child countdowns to bedtime so she can begin to disengage from activities.** Children do not have on/off switches. They need time to transition from one activity to another, especially from daytime energy to nighttime energy. Reading, storytelling, and even humming help slow the pace.

5. **Keep a predictable sequence to the bedtime routine and a regular bedtime to help set your child's biological clock.** Structure creates a peaceful inner rhythm.

6. **Find creative ways to respond to emotional separation issues without compromising essential order.**

Check on your child frequently, particularly when she's quiet, until she truly believes she is safe. Add a simple ritual, like blowing three kisses or sprinkling dream dust on her bed. Make a bedtime photo book with pictures of your child getting ready for bed, sleeping through the night, and waking in the morning, to show her that morning always follows night.

7. **Expect illness, travel, and daytime challenges to disrupt your child's routine for short periods of time.** Allow a few days or a few weeks to reestablish the old order.

BOREDOM

Situation: My child is bored at home. He can't play by himself. He always wants me to entertain him unless he's on the computer or watching television.

Entitlement Issues: More! More! More! Your child needs more because he doesn't know that he has enough—enough stuff, enough imagination, and enough curiosity to fill his time in interesting and satisfying ways.

Entitlement-Free Perspective: Entertainment is the quick fix that never satisfies, just like the junk-food snack that leaves you hungry. A passively engaged child is dependent on external stimulation, while an actively engaged, entitlement-free child uses external prompts to expand his experience. When your child needs you to entertain him, you become the energy source instead of your child. You can easily shift responsibility to your child, who will then play independently for longer periods of time. As you and your child discover his genuine interests, his independence and resourcefulness will flourish. The entitlement-free child will appreciate time to do things that he values, and you might be able to fit in a few adult phone calls. He may always need you, but he won't always need an audience.

ENTITLEMENT-FREE STRATEGIES

1. **Take time to "un-teach" old habits of dependency.** You don't want to withdraw attention cold turkey. It may take a few weeks to practice his new independence in a variety of situations.

2. **Prepare your child for what you want him to do.** Set him up for independence in short intervals and with concrete ideas. Give specific directions: you want him to keep himself busy at the table while you pay a few bills, or to play with quiet toys until you call him for bath time.

3. **Make sure he has what he needs or knows where to get it.** Model the thinking process. If he's doing art, does he have enough supplies and enough variety? If he's playing games, does he have ones that are fun but not too frustrating?

4. **Check on your child before he finishes an activity or gets bored.** You can then assist with transitions to new activities if needed. Don't try to buy yourself extra time only to find that your child is getting into mischief. Be there to redirect him before he exhausts his resources.

HITTING PARENTS
Situation: My child hits me whenever she doesn't get what she wants.

Entitlement Issues: Of course it's wrong to hit, but some children aren't like other kids. You can't reason with your child when she's upset. You can't stop her when she gets out of control. You're hoping she'll outgrow this stage or that she'll stop when she goes to school.

Entitlement-Free Perspective: All children need to learn certain basic behaviors to coexist with other people, regardless of the child's temperament. Physical restraint is at the top of the list. It may take your child a little longer to learn self-control, but you still must actively teach appropriate behavior. It requires vigilance, not reason.

The entitlement-free child doesn't blame someone else when things go wrong, saying "*you* did this to me" or "*you* upset me." She is held accountable for her actions with clear boundaries and alternatives. The entitlement-free child is not left alone in anger to make poor choices. She knows she can count on others to stop her from hurting other people when she feels out of control.

ENTITLEMENT-FREE STRATEGIES

1. **Identify in advance frustrating situations or your child's bad moods.** Anticipate when things are about to fall apart. For example, take your child home from the park before she gets tired, or offer your help *before* she throws the puzzle pieces off the table.

2. **Say yes once in a while, to avoid adding to frustration levels.** Rephrase negative answers without changing the rules. For example, if your child asks to go to Chuck E. Cheese's after school, say, "Yes, good idea. We can go this Saturday with Dad."

3. **Remove yourself physically from your child's reach.** You know when her rage is brewing. Move away *before* she starts swinging, letting her know that hitting doesn't solve problems. If she starts to follow you, tell her to stop where she is and ask her to try to tell you what's wrong. Tell her you can listen when she uses her words instead of her hands. Do not try to hold your child while she hits you. Do not get in her face.

4. **Say clearly, "I'm not going to let you hit me," and mean it.** Show your child in words and body language that hitting holds no power. Stay calm without returning anger with anger.

5. **Teach your child other options when she is ready to lash out at you.** Hitting hands need to wait in pockets until the hitting feeling goes away. Show her that people will listen and try to help her when she's calm.

BICKERING SIBLINGS

Situation: I thought my children would be best friends, and all they do is antagonize each other—in the car, at the dinner table, everywhere. They tease each other constantly and bicker over every little thing.

Entitlement Issues: Parents are supposed to create an ideal world for their children to thrive. There must be a way to make children love each other. Every child deserves to be loved.

Entitlement-Free Perspective: Your child is loved, truly and genuinely, by you. In many ways, that's more than enough. Young children are just figuring out this crazy little thing called love—mostly they love everyone until someone does something they don't like. Typically siblings do a lot of things the other doesn't like, and they can quickly become an inconvenient nuisance. The entitlement-free solution is not to demand that everyone love one another but to teach siblings acceptable behavior in a family culture of respect. You actually begin to teach your children that love isn't based on getting your way. In the end, your children will learn to understand one another better than anyone else ever will. The love you hope for will come from deep insight and caring instead of a well-meaning but unrealistic commandment.

ENTITLEMENT-FREE STRATEGIES

1. **Find one phrase that captures an age-appropriate sibling message for your family.** For example, "You may not always like what your brother does, but I want you to use kind words," or "Brothers are brothers forever—I hope you can work this out." Your expectation is now a family motto for all time.

2. **Without taking sides, get the children to describe the problem (even if you saw everything).** Listen to both sides until everything the children need to say is said. "He hit me." "Her foot touched my foot." "His breath stinks." Get it all. Then proceed to the next two strategies.

3. **Help the children clarify any *real* underlying messages.** Offer your grown-up insight to the situation. For example, "I think you're really trying to say that you're tired and need a little space," or "You look like you're still mad that your sister lost your truck."

4. **Start looking for a workable solution.** Ask the children first, "What can we do about this?" If they can agree on an

answer, give it a try whether or not it makes sense to you. If the conflict is irresolvable at this time, find a temporary solution to keep the peace. Rotate the children's seats in the car so they aren't next to one another. Institute quiet time when conflict is escalating. Make a game of change-the-subject—for the next five minutes, you can only talk about "blue" or "giant green alligators."

CLEANUP

Situation: My child refuses to pick up her toys or clean her room.

Entitlement Issues: Parents shouldn't force children to do things they don't want to do. It creates stress between the parent and child. Besides, a child has more important things to do than menial labor. It's more important for a child to do homework, practice a musical instrument or a sport, and have time for a little reading before bed. The maid can pick up the toys. She gets paid for it.

Entitlement-Free Perspective: A sense of personal responsibility for the things you use is essential, especially for children who are still making basic cause-and-effect connections in the world. The entitlement-free child is personally responsible for her things, for the same reason that Oprah signs her staff's checks and scuba divers carry their own equipment: because then you know that everything is as it should be. An appreciation of hard work also prevents entitlement-free children from taking other people for granted.

Cleanup doesn't have to be a nasty chore unless you present it that way. Given time and planning, cleanup is just the last step in a fun activity. Children who only want the best part of the activity are like children who only eat the frosting and leave the cake. They miss out on some really good cake!

ENTITLEMENT-FREE STRATEGIES

1. **Decide on a realistic plan for your child.** Should she put things away before taking more things out, or should she put everything away an hour before bedtime? When creating your plan, consider your child's play style. Is she easily overwhelmed by all the toys, or excited when creating new games using diverse props?

2. **Make cleanup a game.** Play Beat the Clock and let your child set the timer. Pick up toys according to color or largest to smallest. Get involved. Everyone knows that unpleasant tasks are easier when shared.

3. **Let your child know when cleanup is helpful, so she knows the effect of her actions on other people in the family.** She will feel competent and know that she makes a contribution to the family. Feel free to exaggerate: "Mommy will sleep good tonight knowing all the toys are on the shelves," "I think I heard one of your toys whisper thank you—did you hear it?" or "Nanny told me it's easier for her to find a game when you keep them all together."

4. **Accept approximations of "clean," gradually increasing the amount of responsibility.** If necessary, remove excessive toys until your child is in the habit of cleaning up. It's less overwhelming to take care of five toys and add back a little at a time than it is to sort hundreds of pieces all at once.

Home is the strongest influence in your child's life, the place where he must experiment with rules and expectations. The entitlement-free child thrives with love, security, and guidance at home, where he learns to make mistakes, speak to others, and think for himself. More than a building, home is you. The entitlement-free child is counting on you to create a place for real people to grow.

5

PRAISE AND FEELINGS

- **Make peace with all emotions—happy ones and difficult ones.**
- **Teach your child to express all emotions safely and respectfully.**
- **Make thinking and feeling partners in action.**

Feelings are the cornerstone of entitlement-free parenting. The entitlement-free child experiences firsthand both positive and negative emotions—feelings of love, joy, and trust as well as feelings of confusion, fear, and frustration. A young child does not yet have the language or the sophistication to readily express complex emotions, especially negative ones. But with your help, the entitlement-free child learns emotional mastery, not through overprotection but through age-appropriate understanding. The entitlement-free child begins to recognize her emotions and the emotions of others in everyday family situations.

Your child's inner world is not exactly private. From sunshine smiles to shrieking despair, from chattering enthusiasm to stomping anger, young children do not censor what they feel. You know when your child is happy, and you know when she's spitting mad. Your child's emotions pulse through her entire body. Children gain emotional mastery as they learn to express feelings effectively in words and actions.

At first, emotions are confusing, but with experience, adults learn to accurately identify feelings. You feel a knot in your stomach and learn it's nervousness. You feel your ears getting hot and know you're going to say something you'll regret. Young children easily can mistake one emotion for another. Tired feels like frustration on a busy day. Confusion can feel lonely. And vulnerability can feel scary. How can a child master her emotions when adults can barely figure them out?

You lead your child by keeping a perspective outside of your child's emotional storm; you're the hurricane pilot who flies into the storm to gather important information and never loses sight of the way out. Your child depends on feedback from you and from others. Sometimes hitting makes the hitter feel strong and powerful when faced with unfairness. But hitting also hurts other people. A young child learns to weigh the other person's discomfort against her immediate pleasure by seeing her actions from other people's points of view.

Entitlement-free children don't learn self-control overnight. It takes trust to postpone gratification, and stamina to resist impulsivity. It also takes practice to think clearly under pressure. The entitlement-free child learns these skills and much more in ordinary childhood dramas. The entitlement-free situations in this chapter give your child the opportunity to thrive in a world of emotions as a resourceful problem solver and respectful communicator.

LOVE AND DISCIPLINE

Situation: I tell my child I love her when I'm disciplining her so she'll never question my love.

Entitlement Issues: Your fear that your child will be "without" your love creates a false and confusing sense of entitlement. Your love is deep and ongoing. And yes, at non-discipline times, you can immerse your child in loving rituals that create a sense of security. But your child is not a love-munching machine that must be fed incessantly like a broken parking meter. Allow your child to learn to trust you—to trust that you truly act on her behalf.

Entitlement-Free Perspective: Discipline, limit-setting, and disapproval are appropriate responses to inappropriate behavior and are not about withholding love. Children test the people with whom they have strong, healthy attachments in order to clarify right from wrong and to establish a personal identity. Every time your child pushes against safe and predictable boundaries, she gets a clearer picture of who she is and her place in the world. Your child needs limits in order to grow.

ENTITLEMENT-FREE STRATEGIES

1. **Confidently stand by the rules that are important in your home.** Start with safety rules for potentially dangerous behavior, like not running into the street. Gradually add the rules and routines for meal times and bedtimes. Then include rules to help everyone live together more peacefully: keep toys in your room so we don't trip on them and markers at the table to prevent writing on the furniture.

2. **Teach the rules for new activities.** Rules should be positive directions, not always negative restrictions. Your child is learning *how* at the same time she is learning *what*. Supervise new experiences, using redirection and problem solving *before* inappropriate behavior escalates.

3. **Believe in your right to say no, and accept your child's right not to like it.** You may not always feel smarter than your child, but you can predict undesirable consequences that your child cannot anticipate. As your child grows, you'll even stand back as you allow negative consequences to happen (without saying, "I told you so").

    Include love rituals in your daily routine to give your child reassurance without guilt: a special love song, a tickle game, a secret "I love you" wave, a bedtime promise, or a one-of-a-kind morning greeting.

4. **When disciplining your child, keep communication focused on the behavior.** Additional emotions confuse children and interfere with their ability to hear your message and act responsibly.

"I HATE YOU"

Situation: My child says "I hate you" whenever I tell him to do something he doesn't like.

Entitlement Issues: You're on a wild goose chase to keep your child happy. Entitlement is brewing on the horizon, because you're in an endless spiral of more, more, more. You can only hold disappointment at bay for so long. Eventually your child must feel what he feels—anger, frustration, injustice. When your child says, "I hate you," he is lashing out recklessly and hurtfully. At some point, after he has time to figure out his emotional reaction, he needs to know the force of words on others. There is a better way to express emotions—no one is entitled to dump and spew nastiness indefinitely.

Entitlement-Free Perspective: Here's one of those complex emotions that your child needs to unravel in age-appropriate ways. What is he really feeling? He doesn't like what you say, and he's too angry to articulate what's bothering him. Find the strategies that help your child communicate honestly and respectfully. The entitlement-free child has realistic options when he gets stuck, and he is invested in finding constructive behaviors in problem situations.

Entitlement-Free Strategies

1. **Accept your child's right to protest your requests and decisions, without getting caught up in the situation.** Validate your child by saying, "I see you're not happy about this right now" or "You don't think this is fair, but now isn't the time to talk about it. We can talk about it later if you still want to."

2. **Do not try to convince your child that you are right, particularly when emotions are high.** Your child is not open to reason at this time, which puts you in a position of defending the indefensible.

3. **Focus on the immediate solution instead of getting sidetracked.** What do you need to do right here, right now—get out of a store, leave the party, or go feed the dog while your child calms down?

4. **Make time in the day for open-ended discussions to help your child understand the emotional aspects of a difficult situation.** These talks can be in the car, on an evening walk, or while snuggling in a cozy chair. Start with a simple statement like, "Phew, you looked really upset when…" Time for listening is why under-scheduling your child's day is critical.

5. **Help your child identify constructive alternatives to reactive behavior.** Parents can model problem-solving questions and possible solutions. What helps your child calm down? Throwing a ball against the garage wall, petting the dog, or pretending with toy dinosaurs? What else could your child do when things don't go his way? Offer to plan the activity for another time, find something else that Mommy will say yes to, or think of other things that he can do instead.

FEAR

Situation: My child is afraid of automatic flush toilets, and she knows which stores and restaurants have them.

Entitlement Issues: There isn't any reason to frighten a child unnecessarily. So you drive miles out of the way to avoid the scary flushers. Appeasing a child's fear may seem kind and compassionate, except that it suggests that your child is not capable of handling the situation. Or in entitlement thinking, it suggests that your child *should not have to* deal with unpleasantness. Unfortunately, appeasement often creates a new set of problems, because it establishes a precedent of avoidance. Fear then begets more fear or more elaborate avoidance, because a child never has the opportunity to discover her inner strengths.

Entitlement-Free Perspective: Fear is inevitable in every child's life, because children do not understand cause and effect logically—darkness can "eat" a room, and children can get "sucked down" bathtub drains. But your child doesn't have to face fears alone. Families face difficulties together, and every fear has an age-appropriate response. Don't help your child avoid fears; help her cope with them.

The entitlement-free child learns to ask for help and learns to find solutions to life's difficulties. She's not expected to handle adult situations in adult ways but can trust loving adults to find a child-size solution.

ENTITLEMENT-FREE STRATEGIES

1. **Try to understand your child's fears according to child logic.** All fears are reasonable, even if they aren't rational.

2. **Give voice to your child's fears.** "That's a loud, scary noise." Or, "You weren't ready for the flusher yet." Emotions need to be put into words before you can fully understand and control them.

3. **Give your child both emotional support and a chance for problem solving.** Your child needs an empathetic hug or a hand to hold as well as practical strategies. Think out loud, "What should we do now?" or "What can we do next time?"

4. **Find a solution to help your child face the very real, tangible situation (rather than an ambiguous fear).** You can cover the automatic flush sensor with a Post-It Note or find another way to block the signal. You can study the signal light with your child when she has her

clothes on and you're not in a hurry, and try to understand how it works. If surprise and unpredictability caused the fear, repeated practice will help condition a different response.

5. **Do not rush your child.** Stand by your child with comforting security until she is ready to move on. Impatience will only force your child to retreat or regress.

BEING DIFFERENT

Situation: I told the grandparents not to mention my child's hearing aid so he won't feel self-conscious.

Entitlement Issues: It isn't fair that your child is different and has to wear a hearing aid. People may stare at him, and other children may tease him. He should at least have some peace in his own home. You naturally want to do everything you can to make things easier for him. Unfortunately, this assumes that all kids *should* be a certain way or there's one kind of "normal"—which isn't true.

Entitlement-Free Perspective: It's time to let go of striving for one ideal image of children and childhood. This is a diverse world where an appreciation for one another's differences helps everyone to better understand their own gifts and challenges. Entitlement-free thinking encourages parents to raise children to stand up for themselves and to respect one another. Self-consciousness comes from thinking there's something wrong with being different. Immerse children in the idea that differences are normal.

ENTITLEMENT-FREE STRATEGIES

1. **Model for your child the words and attitude that express acceptance of differences.** When someone in a store or at a story time notices your child's hearing aid, you might casually tell them about it and when your child first started wearing it. If another child is curious, you can explain that it's like the volume on the radio and that it helps but doesn't hurt at all. Encourage your child to talk to other people about his differences rather than be defensive. Keep it fun and interesting.

2. **Respectfully discuss all the ways people are the same and different, such as eye or hair color, language or skin color, and using eyeglasses or wheelchairs.** Expose your child to books where he will see these differences. Visit inclusive playgrounds designed for children with different developmental or physical abilities. Explain the right words for differences in skin color. Show your child how to draw the special shape of his friend's eyes. Notice that the child in the video is singing in a wheelchair.

3. **Answer your child's questions in simple, factual statements.** Help him imagine the other person's experience. What's good about a hearing aid, or a wheelchair? What's fun? What's difficult? Do you think people like talking about being different? Do you think they need any help or can help you in any way?

4. **At some point, you also need to prepare yourself and your child for teasing.** Not everyone understands differences. Maybe there's a way to disarm ridicule with a little silliness or a calm reply: "I'm not perfect, but I'm

fun," or "I've worn this since I was a baby, and I don't feel bad about it."

5. **Most importantly, all children should be taught to speak up for one another against bullies.** A bully has no power without negative attention.

OVERDEPENDENCE ON ONE PARENT

Situation: My child cries when she knows Dad is picking her up from school. She says she wants me to pick her up, but I'm working, and I can't leave in time.

Entitlement Issues: You want your child to be happy like the other kids. Your child deserves what all the other children have. What is that? A mom at home after school, a mom on call all the time, a mom who only thinks of her child? Of course you want to be there for your child. But the entitlement ideal can leave you feeling like you don't measure up.

Entitlement-Free Perspective: Your child is in good hands. You want your child to know that Dad is as loving, as caring, and as capable as Mom. There are certain times when a child prefers one parent over the other. These are wonderful times to spend time with that special parent, but you don't want to fall into a trap of compartmentalizing kids with one parent. Children thrive with exposure to different adult personalities and styles. The entitlement-free child knows that different people can meet her needs in different ways. She also learns how to adapt to different personalities and to communicate her needs to others.

Entitlement-Free Strategies

1. **Confidently explain to your child that she is in good hands.** This isn't a negotiable situation. A simple explanation can become your new family mantra: for example, "Daddy does things his special way, and that's great for you too."

2. **Create an after-school ritual of calling each other at a specific time.** Give your child a quick "mommy fix" without the guilt or drama.

3. **Be a proud working parent.** You are your child's role model for making a contribution to the world outside the family. Know why you work, and discuss the benefits of working to you and to your family. Children need to see their parents as people, not just as parents-to-meet-children's-needs.

4. **Find an adult outlet for any guilt.** It's easy to try to do it all and be it all, all at the same time. Make the choices that are right for your family right now, even if they are less-than-perfect choices. Call a friend. Call your mother. Laugh, cry, scream. Your stress and guilt are not meant for your child.

SELF-IMAGE

Situation: My child is always looking in the mirror and asking if he's fat or if he's handsome. I worry about his self-esteem.

Entitlement Issues: You tell your child he is beautiful and perfect, because you never want him to think otherwise. You never want him to feel "less than" someone else. You hope that if you surround him with an environment of positive praise, he will never feel badly about his appearance or in comparison to someone else.

Entitlement-Free Perspective: The entitlement-free child isn't fooled by artificial praise. Preschoolers and kindergartners can already make accurate comparisons of differences, whether it's one child's creative artwork compared with another's hurried scribble or one child's agile body compared with another's struggling attempt at a sport. The entitlement-free child has a realistic appreciation of strengths and weaknesses. He is taught how to evaluate *image* independently of superficial ideals. The entitlement-free child knows there are many ways to define beauty, strength, and talent. Most importantly, the entitlement-free child is not afraid to compare his strengths and abilities to others, because his abilities are not minimized by someone else's successes or talents.

ENTITLEMENT-FREE STRATEGIES

1. **Emphasize your child's healthy body over an ideal body image—his strength, resilience, ability to heal, what it means to feel good.** Discuss all the ways your child relies on his body every day.

2. **Give your child a sense of responsibility for caring for his body.** Try a simple message like, "Your body is your friend—you take care of it, and it takes care of you." Movement, good food, and rest are choices that feel good. Lethargy and junk food make you irritable and unpleasant.

3. **Watch for unconscious negative messages.** If you are weight conscious, whether you need to lose a few pounds or not, your child will question his weight. If you are

obsessive about exercise, even if you look great, your child focuses on the anxiety instead of the positive action.

4. **Help your child construct a self-image that accurately reflects who he is—size, shape, features—not someone else's ideal image.** Build routines and activities around your child's strengths. Not all children can do the same things well—some are strong, while others are flexible; some are tall, while others are short. Teach your child to appreciate what is unique about his body. Your child's confidence and self-esteem will grow from a healthy environment and a healthy attitude.

PRAISE

Situation: I constantly praise my child, saying things like, "Good job" and "You're amazing." I wonder if she hears me or if she just tunes me out.

Entitlement Issues: You want your child to believe she can do anything and be anything. You don't believe in negativity, especially around children. So you try to create an enthusiastic, positive environment around her. The entitlement child gets into trouble when she believes she can do anything without effort, planning, or hard work. Praise can backfire on you in two ways: first, it creates a false sense of confidence that "everything should be easy because I'm so good"; or second, it obscures a child's real ability, because "everything is perfect." Overzealous cheerleaders get tuned out because they'll cheer for anything.

Entitlement-Free Perspective: Encouragement is stronger than praise and better than criticism. The entitlement-free child knows that caring adults are cheering for her and supporting her, but she also knows that some accomplishments are the result of hard work and commitment, privileges are earned through proven responsibility, and mistakes are not negative, but part of a learning process that builds greater precision and ability.

ENTITLEMENT-FREE STRATEGIES

1. **Recognize your child's strengths with honesty and insight.** Help your child identify her natural gifts and abilities. Be specific: "Did you notice you spent fifty minutes building that skyscraper?" "Those were some tricky spelling words this week—how did you learn them so fast?" or "I counted, and you blocked the soccer ball six times today."

2. **Explain what's involved with "greatness."** Athletes sweat and fail and correct mistakes; dancers and musicians practice, practice, practice; presidents go to college and excel at diplomacy; authors throw away first and second drafts; and sometimes artists aren't recognized until long after they die.

3. **Teach your child to measure her own success by establishing goals and standards.** Ask what she would like to do or to be, and show her how to accomplish that. Find real-life role models to teach and inspire.

4. **Allow your child to make mistakes and learn from them.** Learning always involves risk-taking. In order to learn something new, you must take a chance. Find the edge, fail, and try again. Praise is cheap compared to helping someone learn something difficult.

5. Celebrate effort, time, commitment, personal pride, stamina, and perseverance—not just perfection. Strive for greatness. Don't settle for perfection.

APOLOGIES

Situation: I always apologize when I lose it and yell at my child, because it hurts my child's feelings. I also apologize at other times when he's sad or disappointed at the weather, in other people, or with his predicament.

Entitlement Issues: The entitlement parent apologizes, not because people make mistakes, but because parents shouldn't be less than perfect. The first, you can control; the second, you cannot. The entitlement child grows up expecting a world very different from real life, one where it never rains on picnics and mommies can fly over traffic. He projects a world that matches his desires and rejects the world that denies his wishes. He comes to believe he deserves an apology when-ever the world fails his expectations, keeping everyone on the entitlement hook. Saying you're sorry is also only a quick fix without the extra effort to correct genuine mistakes. The entitlement child then learns to apologize without remorse and without a genuine regard for the other person. You may have seen this child moving through a group of children, saying, "Sorry" over and over as he continually pushes chil-dren out of his way.

Entitlement-Free Perspective: Apologize for mistakes, inappropriate behavior, and accidents. The entitlement-free child will learn, from your example, that people make mistakes and people accept responsibility for mistakes. But the entitlement-free child also needs to learn emotional integrity. Apologizing while repeating the same mistake over and over excuses inappropriate behavior instead of correcting it. People are accountable for what they do and say, and emotions are real, not merely convenient. But parents are not liable for age-appropriate difficulties and childhood unfairness. The entitlement-free child learns to express negative emotions with an empathetic person who can listen without feeling responsible for the child's discomfort.

ENTITLEMENT-FREE STRATEGIES

1. **Apologize for behaviors you have control over.** Do not apologize for things you have no control over. Apologies go hand in hand with responsibility. Did you, in fact, do something wrong? Or is your child simply unhappy about a less-than-perfect situation?

2. **Accept responsibility for your role in discipline.** Set limits, and stand by them. Stop counterproductive yelling, hitting, or emotional tirades as soon as you are aware of them. If need be, walk away first to regain composure. Do not apologize to your child while you are disciplining him.

3. **Accept responsibility for your emotions.** Know what you're feeling, just as you would ask your child to identify his feelings—anger, frustration, impatience, exhaustion, embarrassment, annoyance. Simply say to your child that you need a few minutes before you can speak calmly again. If your child did something wrong, address it. If you overreacted, admit it. But keep the two distinct.

4. **Help your child separate feelings from actions, and help him understand that he makes choices, too.** Your child has choices as to how to act on different emotions in different situations. He can sit with his disappointment until he's ready to do something different. He can think of something else to do to try to feel better. If something isn't right, he can find a way to make it better. He can ask for hugs or help, and someone will listen.

5. **Show empathy without guilt or apology.** The entitlement-free child lives in a world where emotions and actions are held together by personal responsibility. Feelings are brought into the light of day where they can be understood and shared. Loving adults stand strong as the entitlement-free child learns how to express complex emotions. They also practice constantly to be role models of emotional maturity. There are no victims in the entitlement-free household, because every situation comes with a choice. Over time, the entitlement-free child learns to make choices that lead to constructive action and understanding.

6

FRIENDS

- **Remember the simplicity of childhood friendships.**
- **Welcome age-appropriate conflicts as character building.**
- **Practice asking open-ended questions, like, "What can you do now?"**

Friendships are one of the first experiments in entitlement-free behavior. As your child is drawn into a variety of social situations, he discovers a whole assortment of personalities and idiosyncrasies. He meets the child who is more impatient than he is, who cheats to win a game, or who trades in old friends when new ones come along. It's no longer "my way"—it's "my way" meets "your way." Compromises are required. The entitlement-free child appreciates the nuances of individual differences and has the ability to maneuver around unexpected social predicaments. More specifically, the entitlement-free child learns how to communicate and to empathize. He also learns how to choose a good friend and to be a good friend.

The entitlement-free child is not fooled by false entitlement beliefs like, "I like everyone, and everyone likes me." The journey to entitlement-free thinking begins with an honest understanding of childhood friendships. The definition of a friend for young children is very different than for adults. Most childhood friendships begin as entitlement-driven, with Me-Mine-Now. "You make *me* happy; therefore, you are my friend."

To a naturally "entitled" two-year-old, first friends are all about *me*—"I like the color of your shirt, so I'll be your friend" or "If you give me a turn playing with your toy, you will be my best friend." A young child's *best* friend is the person he is playing with *right now.* Adults, on the other hand, expect friendships to persist through time. Once you are my friend, you must be nice to me, remember my birthday, and say loyal things behind my back. For children, the rules are simpler. If I'm mad at you, you're not my friend, at least for the next ten minutes. The entitlement-free parent keeps this kind of kid logic in mind before overreacting to the social dramas of children's playgrounds and parties.

Something else happens in young children's friendships that does not happen among more mature adults. Children experiment with social power by testing how far they can push and seeing who will push back. Social situations become the testing ground for becoming a person. Young children are defining who they are—what does it mean to be a boy or a girl? To be big or small? To be fast or strong? They begin to direct the roles and rules of being together. The soap opera begins. Three girls will be happily taking turns on the slide when you hear those familiar whiney voices announce to a helpless boy, "You can't play with us." Exclusivity prevails. One minute you're "in," the next minute you're "out."

Before they can make better choices, children need caring adult guidance to sort through hurtful messages like, "Go away, I hate you," "I'm not your friend anymore," or "You can't come to my birthday party." The entitlement-free child learns the impact of such words and actions. In the upcoming social situations, the entitlement-free strategies focus on fearless problem solving. These are age-appropriate struggles that prepare your child for a bigger world with diverse personalities and peculiar agendas. The entitlement-free child will learn who is trustworthy and who is not, who is honorable and who is not. He will also learn to live by the qualities he values in others.

BIRTHDAY PARTIES

Situation: My child did not get invited to a classmate's birthday, and I don't think that's nice or fair. I think the school should set a new policy immediately that all classmates must be invited to birthday parties.

Entitlement Issues: You know all of your child's wonderful traits, and there's no reason why your child should be excluded from something that his other friends are attending. Besides, how could you possibly explain this kind of hurtful behavior to a child? Your child will be devastated. Childhood is supposed to be happy. How can a young child face others who will think he isn't as good as they are? You want the school's full support on this.

Entitlement-Free Perspective: Life really isn't fair. It takes a brave and wise parent to try to explain exclusionary behavior. But friendships cannot be legislated. More importantly, you can choose to respond in ways that help your child to weigh the importance of other people's actions and to make independent decisions about the qualities of friendship. Entitlement parenting insulates your child from difficulty and creates a false expectation that other people "owe" him certain courtesies. Instead, teach your child self-respect, even when other people do things you perceive as thoughtless.

<h2 style="text-align:center">ENTITLEMENT-FREE STRATEGIES</h2>

1. **First find out if this birthday party really matters to your child.** Often, adult feelings overshadow the child's perspective. Your child might be disappointed or hurt, or your child might be just as happy not to go. Also, find out if your child wants to go because he wants to attend *the* social event of the year at a cool place, or because he cares about the people. This is the time to consider the underlying values your child is learning.

2. **If your child has been excluded from something he genuinely wanted to attend, begin to unravel an age-appropriate explanation.** What phrases fit the situation that can give your child some handle on it? "The birthday child probably doesn't know you want to be his friend. Let's think of some ways to become his friend." "Maybe the birthday child doesn't think of you as a friend, because you're so bossy when you play together." Or, "Sometimes children do things that really hurt other children—it's hard to be a friend with someone like that."

3. **Be an empathetic role model.** Make time to sit together, give hugs, and listen. Your presence alone acknowledges your child's sadness and your unconditional love. Remember, this is not the time for your child to focus on your feelings but for you to focus on his.

4. **Find other outlets for your sadness and anger over the unfairness.** By all means complain to your spouse, swear to your best friend, and rant to your mother. Talk

to your support network for ideas to empower your child. Just remember this is your child's problem to solve, with your guidance.

5. **Make a plan to help your child consider his options.** What can he say when he next sees the partygoers? Can he check his emotions and ask about their fun, or does he want to tell someone that he was sad? Help your child guess how others will respond—who is kind, who is flippant, who likes to put other children down? Discuss or rehearse possible scenarios. It may take a little trial and error, but you will certainly arrive at a point where your child is satisfied that all has been said or done.

PLAYGROUND FEUDS

Situation: Another child is always rude to my child at the playground—throwing sand, pushing her out of the way, and taking her toys. I plan on telling the other parent that it's time to step in and discipline her child.

Entitlement Issues: *Her* child is ruining *your* child's playtime. The entitlement child came to the playground to have fun; therefore, she should have fun. Someone else's reckless behavior should not negatively affect her positive experience. The world must respond in a timely way to protect the rights of the entitlement child and to rectify the situation. You do not approve of the way the other parent is handling the situation and feel absolutely justified in pointing out the errors in her parenting judgment.

Entitlement-Free Perspective: There is a difference between keeping children safe on playgrounds and parents becoming the playground marshals. Parental supervision is necessary for safety reasons—but there is a difference between protecting children from immediate danger and protecting them from possible danger. Parents must teach safety skills to minimize potential risks and jump in when danger is immediate and real. However, most child-to-child situations warrant a response from the child, not parent intervention. The entitlement-free child learns to stand up to other children or choose another play setting that works for her. She also learns to predict which actions defuse conflicts and which actions escalate conflict.

ENTITLEMENT-FREE STRATEGIES

1. **Ask for your child's point of view before you try to define the problem.** What bothers your child about the situation? Where does your child want your help? Do not assume that what's a problem for you is identical to what's a problem for your child. Listen first.

2. **Help your child figure out the playground personality that is bothering her, instead of feeling intimidated by childhood bravado or by social immaturity.** Is the antagonistic child seeking attention, or is she lacking in self-control? If it's the first, your child can defuse the situation by not reacting to the other child's power plays. If it's the latter, your child can try to redirect the other child: remind her where to put the sand or start a new game of racing to the fence.

3. **Rehearse ways your child can stand up for herself with words, redirection, or personal body language.** Mild-mannered children need guidance to find their "strong voice." Practice saying-it-like-you-mean-it without whining: "Stop that—I don't like that" or "Watch out, you're pushing me." You can also teach your child to change

her social vulnerability. For example, instead of sitting and waiting for the other child to come and take her truck, she can bring a few inexpensive balls and try to create a more mobile dynamic. Finally, show your child how to manifest a confident presence. Stand tall; no slumping. Hold your head high; make eye contact.

4. **Send in the reinforcements.** Be sure your child has a plan of action if things don't go well. It's good to learn that things don't always go well and that there's always a plan B. Show your child how to come to you without looking like a victim surrendering. Or bring another friend, to add strength in numbers or to give your child a peer role model.

SOCIAL AVOIDANCE

Situation: My child doesn't want to go to his friend's house, because another child will be there who calls him names and makes fun of him.

Entitlement Issues: Your child deserves respect from his peers. He deserves to go to social events without worrying about verbally antagonistic bullies. The entitlement child is indignant and self-righteous about how others are supposed to treat him. The entitlement world attempts to finely orchestrate the social world of children in order to prevent bad feelings and victimization. The adults are prepared to intercede or to allow the entitlement child to avoid unpleasant situations.

Entitlement-Free Perspective: Social situations don't have an easy this-or-that answer. Both going and not going to the friend's house could be beneficial for your child, depending on how the solution is presented. Does your child really want to go to his friend's house but feel threatened by a possible adversary? Or can he honestly say to his friend that he prefers not coming when the other child will be there but will happily come another time? The entitlement-free solution focuses on your child making a choice where he is responsible for his feelings and his actions rather than avoiding a difficult encounter.

ENTITLEMENT-FREE STRATEGIES

1. **Help your child deconstruct his feelings to decipher what he really wants.** Does he want to go but is unprepared to face the situation? Or does he choose to spend time in other ways, fully accepting that sometimes you give up something you like in order to accomplish something you believe in?

2. **Help your child rehearse constructive ways to respond to verbal insults.** Practice the three kinds of responses discussed in the previous situation: words, redirection, and body language. Now is not the time for fluffy pseudo-confidence-building praise. Now is the time to "own" skilled social behaviors. Practice all the different ways to say, "Yeah, you must be right. I'm a butthead"—sulking, pathetic, ironic, incredulous, or arrogant. Discuss a dozen alternatives to engaging in the verbal drama (the longer the list, the easier it gets). Alternatives include getting some food, talking to the most popular child in the room, and being ready to entertain other guests with a great joke. And always assume a powerful posture. Playfully show your child any unconscious messages he sends.

3. **Avoidance is not an option, unless it's only a temporary reprieve until your child acquires greater social skills.** He can practice in less threatening situations. It's up to you to gently coax him to keep trying—if this is important to him, that is.

4. **Support your child's principled action if he chooses not to participate in a situation that he finds demeaning.** You still have a role in a reflective discussion about what matters and what doesn't matter. These are the values that will define who your child becomes.

FULL DISCLOSURE

Situation: I'm afraid that if other parents knew my toddler has had a few "biting episodes," they would not want to play with us.

Entitlement Issues: Children's play groups should be conflict-free. Parents with disruptive or hurtful children should be excluded until inappropriate behavior is under control. In order to live up to unrealistic expectations of parents' and children's behavior, parents are forced to pretend that problems do not exist. The entitlement myths are then perpetuated—children are adorable, cute, and nice under all circumstances.

Entitlement-Free Perspective: There is enormous pressure to have a "perfect" child, or at least a child who doesn't hurt other children. The problem is that "biting episodes" do occur in groups of young children, and everyone who participates in play groups is part of an entitlement-free solution. Biting is unacceptable, but no one can eliminate biting behavior instantly. Controlling biting requires a group focus on prevention and managing parent fear and embarrassment.

The entitlement-free goal is to be ready and able to act responsibly when children are not adorable, cute, or nice.

ENTITLEMENT-FREE STRATEGIES

1. **Make a commitment to play groups that are founded on kindness and mutual support.** Consider not participating in groups that do not share responsibility for emerging social skills and age-appropriate challenges.

2. **Identify the problem behavior openly and honestly.** Observe what provokes "biting episodes"—conflicts over toys, spatial proximity, tiredness, frustration, or lack of verbal skills.

3. **Make biting prevention everyone's priority.** Adults should take responsibility to keep children safe and to help children learn social boundaries. Once a biting incident occurs, expect biting to recur anytime for the next month, at least.

4. **Be ready to intervene when children come into biting range, to assist with redirection.** Deflect the biting by saying, "No biting." Make the message loud and clear by saying, "I won't let you bite her. That hurts her."

5. **Speak up for the child who is bitten, but do not treat her like a victim.** Model a strong response to the biter: "Sara doesn't like that! Don't bite her!"

6. **Stay involved in the social-learning moment.** Toddlers need guidance in moving forward from this cliffhanger. Show them specifically how to share space, to take turns, or to move on to another activity.

MAKING COMPARISONS

Situation: I'm embarrassed to host play groups, because our house is so much smaller than those of my child's classmates.

Entitlement Issues: It's natural to want to give your child everything that everyone else has, especially everything his peers have. Too often the entitlement parent tries to live according to other people's standards, with negative results: feigning wealth and status, going into debt, or pressuring spouses to work longer hours. In order to avoid embarrassment, the entitlement parent might host parties in parks or expensive places rather than invite others into a home that doesn't measure up. The entitlement child never learns to value what is his, and he lives in a world of not-good-enough.

Entitlement-Free Perspective: Children survey everything about the world in an endless comparison of what is the same and what is different. Inevitably, your child will notice the size and quantity of other people's things, even if they don't yet understand financial wealth. The entitlement-free parent is prepared to give an age-appropriate answer to her child to satisfy personal curiosity and prepare him to respond to unsolicited comments from others. The entitlement-free child learns gratitude through an appreciation of the true value of what he has, knowing there will always be someone with more, just as there will always be someone with less.

ENTITLEMENT-FREE STRATEGIES

1. **Check your emotions as a parent first.** Do you feel a twinge of jealousy at someone else's good fortune? Are you measuring yourself against someone else's possessions? Family life is hard enough without trying to believe that everyone else around you has it easy. Things are rarely as rosy as they seem.

2. **Take inventory of what you value—people, time, art, books, history, and nature, for instance—so you can confidently articulate a sense of appreciation to your child.** The marketplace excels at assigning value to objects and experiences. Instead, help your child to identify worth according to your family's values. "Our home is small but happy," or "It may not look like a castle, but we treat everyone well in this home."

3. **Teach your child about differences in possessions and values.** Admit that some people measure success with stuff and some people are prejudiced against people who are not part of certain social groups. Give your child the strength and solidarity of a family standing together with pride. Emphasize generosity and respect regardless of material wealth.

"NOT FAIR!"

Situation: My child is constantly saying, "Not fair!" when she can't have or do what other children do. I would mortgage the house to give my child all the advantages that other children have.

Entitlement Issues: You believe that a good parent gives her child the best possible childhood with the best stuff and the best experiences that money can buy. You believe that children with financial advantages are more successful. But appearances are deceiving, and your child is actually "guilting" you into indulgent entitlement. Much of what other children have is simply feeding the entitlement monster, not creating any permanent advantages. As soon as the monster stops being fed, the entitlement child is lost and helpless.

Entitlement-Free Perspective: Of course, the entitlement-free child still tests parents on notions of fairness. But each time the parent stands up for principles and explains the reasoning behind choices, the entitlement-free child learns how to do the same. To a young child, what's "fair" is what I want here and now, like a big piece of my favorite cake. What's "true" is what I choose to believe right now, for example that Santa Claus will bring me presents and I didn't really break that vase, because it was an accident. Social situations are the perfect opportunity to clarify that "fair" is not necessarily "same." To truly be fair, act in your child's best interest and teach her that success can take many different forms.

Entitlement-Free Strategies

1. **Know your limits.** Everyone has them, and even parents with unlimited resources must create artificial limits to rein in children's wild expectations. Use rules and routines to set the precedent for future choices.

2. **Teach value concepts in everyday situations, so you have the principles to draw upon when your child tests you.** Wouldn't it be great to be able to say, "In this family

we are fair and kind every day"? Does someone always get the best seat in the car, the first choice of movies, or the last cookie? Fill up your "fairness bank" long before it's ever questioned. Young children are guaranteed to check it regularly—they are great at keeping score.

3. **Say no confidently and gracefully, knowing that your child isn't likely to respond by saying, "Thanks, Mom—I really appreciate how smart you are."** If your child is not challenging your parental decision making, you aren't making the tough decisions, and your child isn't doing his job of testing the boundaries.

BOSSINESS

Situation: My child is impossible when friends come over to play. He refuses to share his toys. He bosses the other children around, telling them where to sit, what to do, and even when to go home. I'm afraid he's turning into a miniature dictator.

Entitlement Issues: The bossy child becomes an entitlement child when people think he's cute just the way he is, or when they throw up their hands, claiming there's nothing they can do about it. Entitlement parenting makes exceptions because this is the child's home. The entitlement child is treated as the little prince of the family and will not be dethroned by other children. Social skills, like learning to share and following other people's rules, can be postponed until he gets to school. The teachers are better trained to handle these kinds of situations.

Entitlement-Free Perspective: Those bossy personalities may become the CEOs of the future, but childhood is the optimal time to harness those leadership qualities and channel those visions into more mutually gratifying behaviors. Grown-up bosses may choose to act differently, but childhood bosses can at least learn the basics of social graces. The entitlement-free child learns to think of other people's feelings while he's also learning to assert his robust personality. Planning ahead and setting a few reasonable boundaries help to reinforce manners and polite behavior.

Entitlement-Free Strategies

1. **Plan social activities with your child in advance to include the interests of the invited guests.** Agree in advance what's fair: who decides which games to play, how long turns should last, what happens if someone is unhappy. Keep in mind that children find it easier to share toys that have a lot of pieces than giving up one favorite. The classic rule for sharing is like cutting pieces of cake: one child divides, and the other child chooses. Your child brings out the toys he's willing to share; his guests can choose the ones they want first.

2. **Help your child practice seeing things from other children's points of view.** Say, "I don't think it's fun for your guests to always get the second-best toys," or "I could see that Sammy wanted more turns on your bike." Create a signal to remind your child to be more conscientious when you catch him forgetting. American Sign Language for "friend" or "together" is a fun and easy signal for children to understand. (You can view descriptions and videos of the signs at the Michigan State University Communication Technology Laboratory website: http://commtechlab.msu.edu/sites/aslweb/browser.htm.)

3. **Work on your child's emotional skills in advance, so he knows what to do when he feels frustrated or impatient.** Teach him to "stop" (think of a stop sign) before he impulsively tells his guests to go home. Instead, he can say, "Excuse me" and come ask for your help in finding another game to play. If you hear a conflict brewing, step in and guide your child through it, rather than having him get stuck in old patterns.

4. **Establish social rules that you can enforce during play dates.** For example, "You may not tell children to leave when you get bored. If you do, no more play dates this month." Or, "If I hear you screaming at your friends, you'll need a five-minute play break."

   Allow your child to learn from consequences. Remind him that if this is the way he plays with his friends, they will choose not to play with him one day. If all else fails, your child eventually will face the scorn of his friends. So be it. He will then feel the responsibility of his choices and have to work harder to regain respect.

Family and friends are important forums for developing entitlement-free behavior, because they help your child begin to think of someone else's needs and feelings first. Learning to honor different ways of thinking and different personalities opens your child's heart to a diverse world of experiences. Differences often create temporary conflict as your child discovers there is more than one right way to do anything. But the entitlement-free child learns the art of compromise as a natural extension of thinking of others. He understands that his happiness expands because others are happy too.

7

PARENTING IN PUBLIC

- **Expect in public what you expect of your child at home, or more.**
- **Postpone your embarrassment while you handle a parenting challenge.**
- **Redirect, regroup, or remove.**

Parenting in public is hard. Time stops as you imagine a thousand eyes staring at you. Embarrassment is burning a hole in your brain, and you cannot think. You imagine a neon sign flashing over your head: I'M A BAD PARENT, AND I HAVE NO IDEA WHAT I'M DOING. The entitlement child impulsively exploits public vulnerability; the entitlement-free child is stopped before getting the chance.

No one demands compliance of the entitlement child, for fear of upsetting her fragile equilibrium. She is excused from age-appropriate expectations whenever she is tired, sad, or distressed. As a result, she harnesses super-entitlement powers in public settings, creating a scene to get exactly what she wants. Entitlement-free parenting can de-stress this kind of volatile situation. It won't make you or your child perfect—

parenting is uncomfortable and messy at times. You can expect your child to act like an entitled two-year-old sometimes, but you must also accept full responsibility to teach restraint and respect for others. Saying no to a child is not easy, and staying calm takes practice.

The entitlement-free parent faces the fear of doing the wrong thing in public but will be judged far less harshly, because the entitlement-free response teaches consideration for others. The entitlement-free child learns important skills when she behaves in reckless or careless ways in public situations. This skill-building is not accidental but deliberate and can only be learned through repeated practice in public places. She learns there are different expectations in different places, like quiet voices and walking feet. She learns to notice who and what is around her and which behaviors work well in different places.

Anticipation is the best strategy for public entitlement dramas. There are usually warning signs to foreshadow the ensuing meltdowns: You see the crankiness before your child's legs turn into spaghetti walking down the jetway ramp. You aren't hallucinating when the first few peas fly past the waiter five minutes before your child is banging her head under the table. And, of course, you hope against all odds that your child won't splash the giant urn of holy water yet again, but you will be mistaken.

Be honest. You really do know your child. And you *can* be ready for anything she will do. Expect the unexpected, so you aren't analyzing all your options when that "bad parent" neon sign starts flashing above your head. Act decisively and effectively, and be a realist. If your child can't sit still, you won't be able to keep her happy with a couple of books on the plane. If she loves to scream, she won't be able to sit quietly in the grown-up movie. There's absolutely no way your child will act differently if you don't teach her more appropriate options.

Finally, don't allow behavior today that you'll have to "un-teach" next month or next year. Instead, build a foundation of success. Give your two-year-old only small amounts of food in the restaurant, so it doesn't take a SWAT team an hour to clean the mess under the table—then she'll know how to eat from a plate when she's four. Explain to your child that the aisles of the theater are not for running, so she knows it's a special kind of place. Five minutes of appropriate behavior reinforces long-term habits that only get easier with experience and maturity. Twenty minutes of inappropriate behavior is that much more to be "un-taught" another time.

BRIBERY

Situation: I bribe my child with toys if she behaves when we go shopping.

Entitlement Issues: You want to have fun when you're with your child, not listen to constant screaming and whining. You might think it's a bit exhausting to constantly give her things, but it works. Unfortunately, it doesn't really work, because you find yourself reliving the entitlement drama every time you voice an expectation. The entitlement child learns to use bribery as a negotiating tool against you. You become the hostage as your child leverages you: "If you want me to stop, then you must give me something."

Entitlement-Free Perspective: Bribery isn't wrong if it helps your child learn appropriate behavior. The entitlement question rests on whether or not the child *earns* the toy. Entitlement bribes are given in response to inappropriate behavior, like whining or running through the clothes racks. The entitlement child doesn't learn restraint, because she doesn't have to. She lives with a "fixer"—someone who fixes the problem without making any demands on the child. In these situations, bribery is an act of avoidance.

The entitlement-free child is given the opportunity to learn self-control and responsible choices. Earned rewards, in select situations without an undercurrent of panic and bribery, can help your child learn to defer gratification and to manage raw emotions. She also learns about something bigger than "me." She discovers that stores are special places with specific kinds of behavior and that shopping is a purposeful action with a certain protocol.

ENTITLEMENT-FREE STRATEGIES

1. **Plan your shopping trip with realistic expectations.** Two-year-olds have less endurance than five-year-olds. Making "one more stop" in an already overscheduled day will set off a five-alarm tantrum. The smarter-than-the-child parent plans the day to avoid meltdowns.

2. **Communicate your expectations clearly to your child.** Say, "We use inside voices in stores," "You can buy one thing for five dollars," and "Whining won't get you what you want." Expectations grow and change depending on your child's current skill level. Articulating expectations helps give your child focus and helps you anticipate potential challenges.

3. **Find points of interest, not in the sense of "What's in it for me?" but with an understanding of your child's point of view.** Each venture into the world teaches your child how to expand her experience of her neighborhood.

What's interesting to your child about a grocery store or a home improvement center? Is it finding familiar items that you use at home, pretending you're going to the Arctic Circle to buy ice cream, or pushing the shopping cart in a straight line? Find ways to refocus your child's attention on appropriate behavior instead of boredom and bribery.

4. **Keep rewards on a child-size scale.** Expensive toys can create insatiable consumerism. Earning token rewards like stickers or seashells is more effective at teaching deferred gratification. Small increments of money (quarters or dollars) that must be saved for larger purchases are more effective than large amounts that are never enough.

5. **Focus on the skill (waiting, listening, following directions) rather than on the prize.** The entitlement-free child learns pride in her behavior, not in her possessions.

TANTRUMS

Situation: My child regularly has a tantrum in the grocery store checkout line.

Entitlement Issues: The entitlement child can't help it. If the store doesn't want children to have tantrums, they shouldn't put all that stuff there to tantalize them. The entitlement child's behavior is not his fault or his responsibility. The store is pushing children to the limits of self-control. It's the world that's wrong and imperfect.

Entitlement-Free Perspective: The entitlement-free child has tantrums too. But only the first few times. He knows there will be goodies to tempt him in the checkout line—

and he also knows, without any ambiguity, what the adult response will be to a tantrum. Tantrums don't work. They are ineffective strategies to try to get what you want.

ENTITLEMENT-FREE STRATEGIES

1. **Prepare your child for difficult moments.** Talk about what awaits you in the checkout line, and remind your child what kind of behavior is appropriate. Avoid the lecture—ask your child to tell you what he can do in the checkout line.

2. **Engage your child in positive behavior.** Distract him with conversation: read the covers of magazines for funny stories, count the different kinds of candy, or guess how much money the groceries will cost today. Enlist your child's help: double-check the grocery list, pass the groceries, or plan the evening's dinner. Every time your child has a "job," he learns that he makes valuable contributions to the functioning of the family, and he practices skills for future independence.

3. **Prove to your child that tantrums don't work.** Under no circumstances will you give in to the tantrum. Be prepared to get out of line, leave the store, or even ignore your child. Yes, tantrums are rude to other people, but your child will only have one or two before he realizes it serves no purpose.

EATING OUT

Situation: My child is loud and annoying in restaurants. There's no way to have a relaxed meal.

Entitlement Issues: The entitlement child simply refuses to listen. You've tried to teach appropriate behavior, but she just doesn't get it. You will not leave the restaurant, because that would be punishing the rest of the family. Here is an entitlement conundrum: you might believe that leaving the restaurant is giving your child what she wants. The entitlement child wins anyway, because she holds the emotional power to drive you crazy. She gets her way with irresponsibility and disrespect every time she disrupts a peaceful mealtime.

Entitlement-Free Perspective: The entitlement-free child knows that other people's experiences are as important as hers. Enduring a meal fraught with tension is not maintaining the rights of other family members, nor does it benefit the disruptive child. While it may take months before the entitlement-free child masters dining etiquette, the entitlement-free parent sets realistic expectations and avoids accepting inappropriate behavior out of convenience.

ENTITLEMENT-FREE STRATEGIES

1. **Teach table skills deliberately.** Decide what kinds of behavior are expected at the table: sitting until everyone finishes eating (start with ten-minute increments and build up from there for younger children), using utensils for certain kinds of food, and saying "please" and "thank you." Also decide what kinds of behavior are meal-enders: throwing food, gross noises, or teasing a sibling. Teach your child that manners have consequences by stopping inappropriate behavior quickly. Otherwise you'll be setting a new precedent for what's okay.

2. **Practice restaurant manners at home.** Realize that years of mealtimes are more than just feeding your child. They are the standard for how your child eats. Don't make mealtimes a battleground, but don't let your child hold you hostage either. Serve healthy food in a positive setting. Make it your child's responsibility to act appropriately.

3. **Practice with short meals at restaurants.** Public dining heightens mealtime dramas because there's an audience for budding actresses and comics, and because you've invested time and money in the experience. If your child isn't getting it, try shorter lessons. Go out just for appetizers or desserts, to give your child practice under more limited circumstances. Avoid putting yourself in a losing position.

4. **Set consequences.** Don't go out if you're not prepared to pack up the food and leave when the theatrics begin. Your child may ruin your meal once or twice, but it only takes a few serious consequences to end what could become an ongoing problem.

DISRUPTING OTHERS

Situation: I can't believe we were asked to leave the library yesterday when my child was playing during story time. I told those people they didn't understand kids at all.

Entitlement Issues: A library is a public place. The entitlement child has the right to play if he doesn't want to sit for story time. Whatever happened to childhood? There's plenty of time for rules when children get older. Right now, children should have fun.

Entitlement-Free Perspective: Living in a community means playing by other people's rules. The library has the prerogative to set rules for story time as they see fit. If you don't like the rules, take your child to the playground instead, or when your child is not present, calmly discuss with the library ways to improve story time. The entitlement-free child learns how to respect the rules of a situation even when those rules are different from the rules at home.

ENTITLEMENT-FREE STRATEGIES

1. **Ask about expectations in group settings where other adults are in charge.** It's not unusual that rules for groups of children are different from rules at home or unique to individual programs. Some programs might not allow children to snack during story time; others might allow children to take books from the shelf while the storyteller reads; another may insist that all children be sitting for the entire time. "I didn't know" is not a legitimate excuse for breaking the rules.

2. **Help your child be successful in a variety of situations.** If your child is talkative or energetic in quiet settings, find creative ways to help him sit still: give him a book of his own to hold, draw a silly face on his index finger to make a "silent" puppet, run around outside before storytelling begins, or leave after the first story until he learns to sit longer.

3. **Accept that all children do not thrive in all places.** Your child can enjoy books and the library in other ways. He doesn't have to do what all the other children are doing or be at all the same events.

4. **If you have constructive suggestions for the adults in charge, make them in a mature manner, with full understanding that the library may not welcome your insight at this time.** Being respectful is as important as being right. A more engaging storyteller might get hired next year, but your child will learn entitlement-free behavior this year.

5. **Explain the concept of different points of view to your child.** You can say, "Mommy doesn't want to go to Ms. Patti's story time, because she has the quiet rule." Avoid fault-finding and compounding frustration. Your child then has a choice if he wants to consider changing his behavior in order to go, without being confused by adult emotions.

ADULTS ONLY

Situation: Of course I'm bringing my child to the black-tie wedding.

Entitlement Issues: The entitlement child tells adults how to make adult choices. You may wonder, why not share this experience together if your child says she doesn't want you to go without her? It's only natural that she's looking forward to getting her hair done at the salon and wearing a beautiful new dress too. The entitlement child lives in a magical world where wishes come true and adults always do what you say.

Entitlement-Free Perspective: Children do not decide who attends invitational events. Entitlement-free parenting teaches children to honor the wishes of the host or hostess. The entitlement-free child will experience disappointment, and you might have a better time if your child attends the event. But you must also respect other people's positions, if for no other reason than for your child to learn that other people think and feel differently.

Not only will hosts of adult-only events be relieved, but you may also gain valuable time to be an adult person. Excluding children from certain events and experiences rebalances the needs of the adults in the family. Depending on the age of the child, she may not understand why she can't attend. It's enough to explain the difference between child-friendly places and grown-ups-only places.

Entitlement-Free Strategies

1. **Explain the concept of "for grown-ups," "for mommies," and "for parents only."** Use clear, definitive statements such as, "This is just for Mommy. I'll miss you too." Do not ask for your child's permission to create time without children.

2. **Accept that your child may not like this news.** She might be angry, jealous, or even a tad manipulative (as in "You can't leave me! My stomach hurts"). This is an opportunity for your child to survive a little unhappiness and still thrive. Emotional maturity is the ability to master unsettling emotions.

3. **Use descriptive emotional vocabulary and creative problem solving.** "Looks like you feel sad because you're not included tonight. Can you think of something fun to do tonight with Grandma?" Or, "I think you want to get all dressed up like Mommy. Would you like to get dressed up and have a party at home tonight, or another night when Mommy is home?" Show your

child that there are other ways to meet her needs, and she will learn flexibility too.

4. **Advocate for your own family-friendly preferences in other ways, such as at your events or on parenting message boards.** Host family events of your own to show others how wonderful they can be. Do not criticize someone else's preferences or flagrantly disregard their wishes.

AIR TRAVEL

Situation: I don't think it's reasonable to ask my child to sit buckled in an airplane seat for three hours.

Entitlement Issues: The needs and wants of the entitlement child should be everyone's priority. Strapping in a child against his will is pure torture to the child. As the parent, you might even want to advocate for your right to decide the best way to keep your child safe in an airplane.

Entitlement-Free Perspective: Confining an active child, whether it's in an airline seat or to an IV in a hospital, is especially difficult for parents of energetic children. Some instances seem necessary, while others appear arbitrary. The entitlement-free perspective operates on an assumption of cooperation. Travelers on a plane are a temporary little society that must function together for a short period of time. This might seem like a contradiction when each passenger moves in a self-contained bubble with no need to interact with anyone else on the plane, but respect is still essential.

Children acquire self-control and respect in these kinds of demanding situations, whether the demands are right or wrong. Once again, as in the earlier situations, the entitlement-free child is learning how to function in a variety of settings. Children who are taught to only follow the good rules learn to challenge *all* rules, because in a diverse world there are few universally applicable rules. Entitlement-free children learn to respect rules that are important to other people and understand the importance of mutual respect.

ENTITLEMENT-FREE STRATEGIES

1. **Practice, practice, practice.** Seatbelts are not optional in cars, just as they aren't optional in planes. Help your child transfer car skills to plane skills by noticing all the similarities between the two. If you truly expect resistance on the plane, play "airplane seat" at home by having your child practice sitting in his car seat while he watches a DVD, plays a sticker game, or colors pictures.

2. **Know your child.** As with other acts of childhood resistance, it may not be about the seat at all. Resistance can be based on attention-getting, pushing emotional buttons in a public setting, or simply the stress of changes to the normal routine, including being tired, hungry, or cranky. Most people are uncomfortable sitting on planes. You need a little of your parental wisdom to fortify your child's stamina in a trying situation.

3. **Model effective problem solving with "what else" thinking.** You can't change the airplane seatbelt rule. *What else can you do?* Surely, there's something good in your purse that is usually off limits to your child. Adults play poker with dollar bills; children can count the pairs and triplets in the serial code. *What else?* Pull out the map in the back of the in-flight magazine. *More?* "What

else" is a never-ending game that will drive you crazy long before your child exhausts the possibilities.

4. **Plan ahead next time.** Get your child involved before you leave home. Teach him to pack his own in-flight goody bag with games and snacks. Build anticipation for airplane-seat games that will distract him from his temporary confinement: cloud games based on the book *It Looked Like Spilt Milk*, sticker books, or mini photo albums.

OBJECTIONABLE ENCOUNTERS

Situation: I don't know what to say to my child when she asks questions about the mentally challenged ticket-taker at the local movie theater. She knows he's different from other people she knows. I think she might even be a little scared.

Entitlement Issues: Disabilities are a difficult topic for young children to understand. Children can't understand why this person is acting strange, and it frightens them. It's just a night at the movies, not the time or the place to discuss complex subjects. Therefore, entitlement parents prefer not to expose their children to things that disturb them.

Entitlement-Free Perspective: Children are naturally observant and curious. The entitlement-free child is rewarded for asking questions, even ones that make adults uncomfortable. She learns that adults are willing and able to address fears about the unknown or unfamiliar in direct, age-appropriate ways. Adults help the entitlement-free child learn about the world as it is, not as a sanitized version of real life.

Do not try to predict the distress of your child in order to avoid indelicate situations. You can answer any question or address any feeling as it arises. Believe in the ability of your child to find ways to personally integrate complex ideas and feelings.

ENTITLEMENT-FREE STRATEGIES

1. **Wait before anticipating problems.** Children often take situations at face value when adults expect profoundly difficult questions. Your child may not have any questions or concerns.

2. **Watch your unconscious assumptions and body language.** Do you say hello to the person at the concession stand but not the ticket-taker? Do you sometimes feel annoyed that you have to deal with this person's quirks? Your child senses your emotional ambiguity long before you do. Clarify your adult discomfort separate from any possible reaction from your child.

3. **Be ready with simple explanations for your child.** Talk to your spouse, friends, and peers to find phrases comfortable for you. For example, "You're right—he acts different than other grown-ups. He talks slower, and he always says something funny about the movie." Or, "He was born with something called Down syndrome, but he still has feelings like you and me."

4. **Follow your child's lead.** It is okay to say, "I don't know," or "Let's find out." Children's questions are original and genuine: "Is his mommy like us?" or "Did he go to school?" Answer honestly and simply. Your child will ask more questions if she needs more information.

5. **Teach sensitivity even when you're not sure what's politically correct.** Children say the darndest things. They ask loud questions. They point, stare, and make

faces. But the most offensive behavior often comes from acting as if the other person isn't there or can't hear you. Tell your child that the other person can hear her and that it hurts people's feeling to talk about them. Feel free to apologize to others when your child is rude. Whisper that you can talk about it later, and do so.

PLACES OF WORSHIP

Situation: Other people seem to think that children should be seen and not heard in weekly religious services.

Entitlement Issues: The entitlement child has just as much right to attend services as anyone else. You may have tried children's services but found they aren't always convenient for your family. If places of worship want families with young children to participate, they need to find ways to meet the needs of families, not vice versa. They should be happy that your child is coming to service, instead of making it more difficult than it already is. Besides, this is supposed to be a religious place—can't *they* show a little understanding?

Entitlement-Free Perspective: Religious places are not always the most child-centered places, particularly adult services that are highly ritualized and involved. The exuberance and spontaneity of children is often out of place in this context, possibly misinterpreted. The entitlement-free perspective shifts the question from "What can you do for me?" to "What can I do for you?"

Teach your child that religious places warrant more respectful behavior than secular places. Be informed as to the special meaning of the religious places, and know what special behaviors are appropriate if you plan to attend, like wearing a kippah or bowing before the altar. The entitlement-free child learns to appreciate this unique place through small, realistic expectations.

ENTITLEMENT-FREE STRATEGIES

1. **Visit places of worship on off-times, prior to or after congregational meeting times.** Children do better in structured settings when they know what to expect and can practice the behavior in advance. Explain to a child the appropriate behavior when the Torah is taken out of the Ark or how to walk in a communion line.

2. **Help your child transfer the information he learns in child-friendly services to adult services.** Transferring a routine from one context to another is not automatically transparent to a child. Take some extra time to explain what's similar and what's different, and clarify the expectations in both situations.

3. **Quietly engage your child during services.** A child's prayer book may hold his interest better than adult materials. If he's getting antsy, gently orient him to something interesting happening around him, particularly something happening *next*. Your child will be in awe of your superpower to predict the future. If your child is quiet and happy twiddling his thumbs, let him be.

4. **Have a realistic plan B for exceptionally long services, like Palm Sunday or Yom Kippur.** Prepare your child by discussing what to do if his stomach growls or if he's tired of standing. Believe he is capable, but watch for the warning signs that he's going to fall apart.

5. **Make a connection between weekly, monthly, or annual religious services and your child's usual routine, like books, bedtime prayers, and mealtime blessings.** Your child has a better chance of "getting it" if it's familiar and repetitious.

Parenting in public has unique challenges that can open your child's eyes and heart to new experiences. There will always be blips along the way, and everyone is guilty of an unintentional faux pas once in awhile. Focus on respect and personal responsibility, and most people will appreciate your sincerity. Public scenes, whether embarrassing or infuriating, are handled more diplomatically when you are an entitlement-free champion at finding those win-win solutions for everyone.

8

SCHOOL

- **Explain how school is different from home.**
- **Make a personal connection with teachers, class-mates, and school staff.**
- **Let the school handle problems at school, and follow their example.**

Your child's first school experiences are exciting and full of wonderful discoveries. They are also nurturing and full of love. Learning is personal, and school is your child's venture into structured relationships outside of home and family. School is an extension of your home, but it is not home. Yes, someone will be there to hold your child's hand when his confidence wavers or to help him when he's confused. But school also operates differently from home by trying to meet the needs of many children and families.

Sending your child to school is an act of trust. You are sharing your child with new people who are there when you are not. You must believe that the school personnel can make good decisions without your continuous input, from the scheduling to the curricula and everything in between. It's important to let go—of your child, of absolute control, and of one right way of doing things, just like you did when you first left your infant with other family members who did things differently than you.

Schools are not perfect for the same reason that parents and children are not perfect. People make mistakes. They misunderstand, misinterpret, or miscalculate. A school represents multiple perspectives and celebrates compromise for the benefits of living in a cooperative community. Expect responsible decision making and mutual regard from your child's school. An entitlement-free perspective acknowledges the needs of every child but listens respectfully to what's beneficial for the classroom and community.

As your child's relationships expand, new personalities will influence your child's moods and behavior as well as his goals and attitudes. Your family will repeatedly redefine itself in response to outside influences. These are opportunities to grow in an entitlement-free world. Diversity enriches your child's experience with exposure to new ideas while simultaneously clarifying old values. The entitlement child expects *his* way to be everyone's way, or *his* way to have priority over other ways. The entitlement-free child is continually learning who he is and who he is not, what he believes and what he does not.

The entitlement-free child is eager to learn new ways of interacting with others at school, whether it's raising his hand to speak or setting a table for classmates. He learns to manage not being first every time, sometimes being second and sometimes being last. Some parts of the school day will be his favorite, but he willingly tries other things too. Some people will be just like the people at home, while others might seem a bit strange at first.

School brings children and families together with shared interests. The entitlement-free child knows that self-respect and respect for others are perfectly compatible. The upcoming situations give you opportunities to prepare your child for a diverse world of mutual respect and problem solving.

PROBLEM WITH THE TEACHER

Situation: Last year my child loved school, but not this year. I think he doesn't like his teacher.

Entitlement Issues: School should be a positive experience, especially for young children. The school should want all children to be happy and thriving, especially at the prices they charge. This problem can't be the child's fault, since he was so happy last year. The school should remedy the situation immediately by placing your child in another class that better meets his needs.

Entitlement-Free Perspective: Before rushing in to change the problem teacher, it may be worthwhile to evaluate the situation more thoroughly. The teacher should be professional and capable, which you can discuss with the school administrator, who can provide ongoing support and training. But children often like or dislike teachers based on personal idiosyncrasies or on parental attitudes toward the teacher. While learning is personal, it is not a personality contest.

Children can learn important things from teachers who are either warm-and-fuzzy or strict-and-demanding. You can help the entitlement-free child understand that all teachers are loving and want to help him learn. Also, have an open discussion with the teacher so that she can learn from your perspective and you can learn from hers. Make an effort to listen, to better understand individual strengths of your child and his teacher.

Entitlement thinking believes every year should be a perfect year. That's not possible. A special teacher is a rare and wonderful gift, like those one or two special friends in a lifetime. Treasure those special teachers by staying in touch, and know that few others can compare.

ENTITLEMENT-FREE STRATEGIES

1. **Help your child express his feelings about his teacher.** This is a time for information gathering and clarification. Try not to react with judgments of right or wrong or defensiveness. Repeat back your child's feelings: "You were scared when Ms. Beth…" or "You were upset when…"

2. **Help clarify what's bothering your child.** Sometimes children react negatively to changes in appearance or hairstyle, quick or slow movements, accents or loudness. Sometimes it isn't about the teacher at all. A child might miss an old, familiar classroom, last year's pet hamster, or a friend that's no longer in the school. Use your adult logic and intuition to understand your child's thinking.

3. **Support the teacher before arriving at a conclusion with partial information.** Your child is watching your reaction to his problem—is his problem manageable or overwhelming? Will it be compounded by your anger or fear? Show your child that you trust the teacher's ability. The teacher may have creative solutions, like spending some one-on-one time with your child or finding your child a classroom buddy. Discuss your child's feelings and possible solutions with the teacher or administrator privately.

4. **Teach your child to adapt to changing classroom routines.** Different teachers have different rules and different styles. Your child does not have to change to please everyone, but he may need to learn some new behaviors. Reemphasize new classroom expectations at home: "Ms. Beth wants one child to pass out the instruments. Last year everyone got their own. Change is hard, but you can remember if you try."

5. **Use home activities to counterbalance challenging school situations.** If this year's teacher is strict, plan unstructured after-school time. If this year's teacher is a little on the flaky side, supplement with more challenging after-school time. Instead of expecting school life always to be "one right way," expect school life to be fluid and changing within the acceptable boundaries of your school choices.

CHOICES AND NON-CHOICES

Situation: My child says she doesn't want to go to preschool today, so I let her play hooky. After all, it's only preschool.

Entitlement Issues: Decisions are made for the entitlement child based on what the child wants at this particular moment. If the child says she doesn't want to go to school, why should she? The entitlement child's mood and immediate wishes take priority over previous commitments or a waiting class of teachers and peers.

Entitlement-Free Perspective: Try to maintain a delicate balance between flexibility and rigidity in your parenting decisions. While special occasions are a wonderful way to break up routines, you can also enjoy exceptions without compromising the integrity of the routine. But make sure to guard against going too far or giving too much.

Children, being children, do not always have a sense of limits. Sometimes they don't know what they really want. An entitlement child starts to enjoy the power of dictating adult decisions. Though she would be very happy at school, she doesn't feel like getting dressed right now, so she makes a Me-Mine-Now decision that affects the entire day. She didn't know school was optional, and now anytime she doesn't feel like getting going in the morning, she exerts this inappropriate power. The entitlement-free child learns to master temporary inconvenience, because an adult guides her to a better decision.

Entitlement-Free Strategies

1. **By all means, break the routine once in a while and have fun with your child.** Just watch out for the slippery slope when rules and routines become meaningless. How much is too much? Consider: Is your child making the decisions instead of you? Are you frustrated by your child's unpredictable choices? Is the school telling you that your child is missing out on significant group activities?

2. **Teach a sense of commitment.** Small commitments are age-appropriate and child-sized, not superfluous and easily disregarded. Explain to your child that the teachers and her friends are waiting for her. Help your child know that she makes a difference to the functioning of the class. Your child develops a sense of competence knowing that school is not the same without her.

3. **Teach responsibility.** Going to school is your child's "job." Hopefully it's a child-friendly, meaningful place and not a nasty obligation. Even dream jobs require some discipline. Don't give your child options on ordinary gotta-go-to-school days.

4. **Build your child's self-discipline by working through don't-feel-like-it moments.** Let your child know you're there to help her. Save the rest of the DVD until later, find her shoes, and call Grandma from the school parking lot instead of leaving late from home. Focus on something positive at school to alleviate the stress of giving up something fun here and now. Take a book to show the teacher, take a picture of the Lego castle built this morning, or put a mystery surprise in her lunchbox.

5. **Keep a calendar of school days and home days in a place where your child can see it.** Your child will feel a greater sense of control over her schedule when she can count the days "in" school and "out" of school. Use the calendar to mark upcoming activities so your child has a concrete reference for the things she likes to do.

WHAT TO WEAR
Situation: My child wants to wear his pajamas to school.

Entitlement Issues: Parents have to choose their battles, and there's really no harm in wearing pajamas to school. Some children are spontaneous and creative. Schools should honor a child's free expression.

Entitlement-Free Perspective: The difference between entitlement and entitlement-free thinking is not in the actual decision made. The difference lies in attitude and awareness. The entitlement child runs the show, and other people make excuses for the behavior. The entitlement-free child learns to live according to the expectations of a particular school community. Here are three different school perspectives on pajamas in school:

- Most preschools have "pajama days" when the entire school shares in the silliness of doing something out of the ordinary. But there has to be an ordinary for there to be exceptions.
- Some schools encourage individual expression and have no problem with pajamas, Halloween costumes, shoes or no shoes, or any other seasonal accessories. If this isn't your school's philosophy, it's important to respect school culture, not stridently assert individual rights.
- Some schools will offer parents the option of bringing a child to school in pajamas to avoid power struggles over dressing at home. But this is a shared decision and cannot be thrust upon the school without the school's consent.

ENTITLEMENT-FREE STRATEGIES

1. **Start with a school reality check.** How would you describe the school's social climate? If it's relaxed and flexible, pajamas on Monday might be no big deal. If the policy is uniforms only, the school may prefer that you handle this situation at home. If you're stressed and confused, call the school and ask.

2. **Take full responsibility for your decision.** Do not tell your child "the school said no" while you're playing the innocent "nice parent" at home. Your child needs to see

you accountable for your decisions. You can disagree and still accept responsibility to follow the rules. Should you disagree with school policy, you can say, "I don't mind if you wear pajamas, but the school does."

3. **Help your child let it go and move forward.** It's easy to get stuck in a "what I want" moment. Look for a creative compromise instead. For example, bring school clothes in the car to change into before going into school. This might give your child that little extra time he needs. Buckle the pajamas in a car seat for a fun ride to school, or tuck them in your purse. This might be silly enough to diffuse the moment. Think of other times when your child can wear pajamas in the car, like going to Grandma's or on a pajama ride to look at the stars.

4. **Teach flexibility through day-to-day practice.** Most likely, your child's behavior is not really about the pajamas. Pajamas are fun, but your child is probably struggling with transitions or possibly testing his options. Ending one thing and starting another is developmentally challenging for children (as it is for adults who know how to enjoy a perfect moment). Little compromises encourage flexibility, while frequent concessions encourage rigidity.

TEACHER'S ATTENTION

Situation: There's a child with a behavior problem in my child's class who needs constant time and attention from the teacher.

Entitlement Issues: Children who are disruptive should not be permitted to penalize the other students who "fit into" the group. You want your child to get the most from her school experience and from this particular year, but that can't happen when other children's behavior is out of control.

Entitlement-Free Perspective: Entitlement-free thinking looks for every opportunity to make classrooms inclusive experiences with a diverse representation of children. It strives to find effective strategies to manage difficult situations before opting for the quick fix that removes the problem or eliminates conflict.

Rather than see the entitlement-free child as penalized by someone else's challenges, the entitlement-free child learns to empathize with another person. She learns to make a constructive contribution to the situation either by better managing her own behavior or by giving age-appropriate assistance to the group. Once again the cohesiveness of the group is given equal priority to the needs of one individual.

Entitlement-Free Strategies

1. **Discuss your concerns with the teacher.** Confirm with the teacher that your child's classroom needs are being met. If your child's needs are not being met, discuss constructive solutions with the entire class in mind. Become part of a solution instead of compounding the problem.

2. **Help your child understand the other child's behavior.** Clarify the situation with age-appropriate descriptions. For example, "Sometimes Max is loud when the other children are trying to be quiet. It's hard to pay attention then." Or, "Sometimes you have to wait for the teacher to help you when she's busy with Max."

3. **Avoid using labels.** Labels often fail to acknowledge the child behind the behavior. You can set an example by speaking respectfully about other children even when their behavior is inappropriate.

4. **Discuss constructive options with your child.** Your child doesn't always know there are many other good choices she can make in these situations. You can clarify ways to keep busy, ways to help the teacher by being independent, or ways to help the other children. Help your child to find solutions. Ask, "What else can you do when the teacher is helping Max?"

CLASSROOM SCHEDULE

Situation: The teacher wouldn't let my child finish his art project today.

Entitlement Issues: You child was not disturbing anyone. He politely asked for more time because he wanted to finish something he started. You expect teachers to be more sensitive to the needs of children, especially when the teacher's actions proved to be very upsetting to your child.

Entitlement-Free Perspective: There are at least two sides to every story. The teacher may have been right or wrong, but either way, the entitlement-free child is given the opportunity to see another person's point of view, to communicate respectfully, and to recover from disappointments. The teacher might have had a bad day or a reasonable justification. The entitlement-free child learns to look beyond his needs and accept that other people make decisions, good and bad, that affect him.

1. **Help your child remember what happened before and after the incident.** There are many possible aspects to this situation. Did the teacher already give the child additional time? Did the class need to leave the room, and the teacher could not leave the child unsupervised? Did the teacher say the child could come back to the project at another time? Has the teacher been encouraging the class to finish projects on time? By discussing the possibilities, you also teach your child how to gather relevant information for understanding complex situations.

2. **Find a reasonable resolution.** Is your child satisfied, having discussed the situation with you? Can your child ask for time tomorrow to finish the project at school, or bring the project home to finish? What can your child do to solve the problem without you rescuing him or usurping the teacher's decision making?

3. **Create outlets for disappointment.** If disappointment is part of life, the entitlement-free child needs to be free to express disappointment without upsetting the adults too. Empathize with your child by saying, "That must have been difficult to stop before you were finished," or "I wouldn't have wanted to stop either." Children need to be heard by adults who are strong and comforting. Be ready to comfort with a cup of hot chocolate or a long walk without needing to "fix it."

MEAN TEACHER

Situation: My child complains that the teacher gives her mean looks.

Entitlement Issues: Children should be taught with love and kindness, not with negative expressions and harsh expectations. Parents have the right to demand that teachers create a positive environment so children can learn easily and comfortably.

Entitlement-Free Perspective: The first response to an entitlement child's complaint is indignation—how dare *you!* It is certainly imperative that the teacher act professionally, but instead the first reaction should be to listen for more information. If a child has not seen adults set limits before, he may misinterpret "serious" as "mean." The teacher may in fact be calm and loving while communicating, "This is the last time I'm asking students to take their seats."

Help your child talk openly about situations that make her uncomfortable. Assure her that nothing bad will happen if she asks Ms. Jill if she's angry. It takes maturity to remember to ask Mom questions after a busy day at school. Dad might offer a different angle. The entitlement-free home is a place for curiosity, fact finding, and hearing different points of view.

ENTITLEMENT-FREE STRATEGIES

1. **Ask open-ended questions for more clarification.** For example, "What does 'mean' look like?" "What do you think Ms. Jill is trying to say?" Or, "When does Ms. Jill make her mean face?"

2. **Involve your child in active problem solving.** "What provoked the teacher's behavior?" "Does Mommy ever give those kinds of looks?" "Is there anything you can do to avoid getting 'the mean look'?" "Do you think there's another way for teachers to act?" "Which way do you like better?"

3. **Build emotional stamina.** The entitlement-free child has a choice when responding to another person's feelings. Sometimes she changes her behavior when she realizes she's acting inappropriately; other times she might decide she didn't do anything wrong. She learns to stand confidently outside of minor classroom dramas.

4. **Create opportunities for random conversations.** Children usually have little to say when asked, "How was your day?" They need gentle prompts to get started. Does a particular story character remind you of your child's teacher? Does your child see the similarity? Or can she guess what flavor of ice cream Ms. Jill would like? You create a social-emotional-cognitive map of the world for your child when you make associations in your child's experiences.

CELL PHONES

Situation: The school does not permit children to bring cell phones to school.

Entitlement Issues: Cell phones are an extra layer of protection in a violent and unpredictable world. The school has no right to limit your child's access to his parents, especially in times of emergency. Your child can and will keep the cell phone turned off during class time, but your child must be able to call you if and when he needs to.

Entitlement-Free Perspective: Schools often set policy guidelines based on group behavior, not on individual behavior. While there may be numerous good reasons for *your* child to carry a cell phone, problems escalate when everyone is carrying a phone. The school must make decisions based on the most effective way to operate all day, every day. The advantages of you being contacted directly by your child may not outweigh the disadvantages and nuisance of student cell phones.

Teach your child to survive and thrive without on-call parent participation. He'll learn that he will be safe in emergencies and wait to discuss school transgressions until he gets home. The entitlement-free child can manage his behavior and his emotions away from the safety net of home and family.

ENTITLEMENT-FREE STRATEGIES

1. **Allow your child to focus on school while at school, be with his friends, and handle the situations that arise with the resources at hand (without you).** He can learn to delay the immediate satisfaction of sharing or complaining until after school hours.

2. **Trust the teachers and the administrators to be your eyes, ears, and hands.** Be informed about emergency contact procedures, keep your contact information up to date, and return calls promptly. If desired, rehearse safety procedures with your child by explaining how he should follow school procedure and how you will be informed, with reassurances that you *will* be there if there's a true emergency.

3. **Enjoy the bonus of not being at your child's immediate call.** Your child is learning to ask for help from other people and to work and play independently from you. You may need to redefine your role as well. Enjoy the additional freedom—your child still needs you in thousands of other ways.

OVER-INVOLVED PARENTS

Situation: I stayed up all night finishing my child's science project for the Open House event at school.

Entitlement Issues: You want your child to be successful and to receive public recognition for being creative and talented. You were simply carrying out your child's vision to help her accomplish her goals. You had to help with the details, because your child would not have been happy with anything less.

Entitlement-Free Perspective: The entitlement child might take pride in *your* work but she will never confuse it with pride for *her own* work. The entitlement child experiences a false sense of pride because she knows she was not responsible for the project on display. The praise and compliments are not really hers to enjoy. The entitlement-free child faces struggles to accomplish a task she can truly be proud of. Her hands-on effort leads to in-depth thought and greater problem-solving skills. Experience teaches her that things do not always go as planned from design to implementation. She confronts obstacles, invents solutions (often through trial and error), and manages it all within specific time constraints.

There is no substitute for authentic effort. The entitlement-free child knows what she accomplished, even if it doesn't look perfect. Her effort is "enough," even in comparison to others' original work. If she wants to do more next time, she can.

ENTITLEMENT-FREE STRATEGIES

1. **Celebrate your child's original work for her unique effort and talents.** Projects of any kind involve a learning curve of time, planning, mistake making, and

finally mastery. Focus your praise on effort and accomplishment; otherwise your child will always expect easy, automatic success.

2. **Allow your child to experience natural consequences.** If your child's work is good, she will witness genuine praise. If your child's work is lacking, she will experience an honest reaction. Help your child put evaluations in a constructive context. For example, did someone else have a really good idea that your child didn't think of? Or could she have spent more time on one area of the project and less on another?

3. **Differentiate your child's personal satisfaction from public opinion.** Ask your child if she is proud of her work before hearing other people's opinions. Give due weight to your child's goals and accomplishment. The entitlement-free child will discover where the truth lies between her personal appraisal and a public appraisal.

4. **Prepare your child for public comparisons.** Discuss in advance whether your child might be disappointed if others don't think her project is the best. Give her strategies to gracefully handle the moment. Plan to celebrate your child's personal accomplishment afterward with cake and ice cream. Talk about ways to share and congratulate another child's success.

School is your child's first community, welcoming him with miniature furniture and miniature freedoms. It's a place created especially for child-sized bodies and oversized hearts. It is one of those rare places where the little people outnumber the grown-ups. As such, the rules are different, the routines are different, and the expectations are different.

School is a place that must juggle a variety of needs, interests, and personalities. Your child is an individual among many. He is both unique unto himself and the same as many other children. Patience and perspective are required to help the entitlement-free child master this new world. A good school has an obligation to celebrate every child. As a result, each child learns respect and generosity.

9

EXTRACURRICULAR ACTIVITIES

- **Make realistic choices that you and your child can live with.**
- **Follow through on your commitments.**
- **Teach a team perspective—winners, losers, roles, and rules.**

Extracurricular activities pose a new set of challenges and contradictions for entitlement-free parents, inundating them with choices. Consider how you choose after-school and weekend activities. Is pleasure more important than skill building? Is price more important than convenience? Is it ever okay to give in to peer pressure? The variety of options raises important entitlement issues regarding how many activities are enough, whether cost should matter if something is affordable, and how to choose one activity over another.

Extracurricular decisions also involve confusing contradictions, from choosing the right activity to figuring out the right level of commitment. One choice eliminates another as you decide whether to encourage your child's well-rounded personality or train a sharp-focused superstar. One parent opts for the karate class to encourage his future scientist to be less bookish and less clumsy, while another parent strives to focus the natural talents of her future Olympian. Then, after you enroll in these voluntary activities that supposedly add to your child's quality of life, you get to decide if it's okay to miss a class here and there, or if quitting is an option when fun stops being fun. Whatever you decide, some other parent will make the opposite choice. The entitlement-free perspective shows you how to live by your choices in a world of diverse interests and ideals.

The entitlement-free child knows that Me-Mine-Now are not criteria for making good decisions. With your guidance, she learns to consider the rules and expectations of different situations. Most activities include some length of commitment—from a few hours of not doing something else to months of showing up somewhere on time in order to play or practice. The entitlement child flitters and dabbles, starting a dance class just to wear the costume or rushing to be first to buy the newest sports equipment. The entitlement-free child can sustain a commitment, because she likes what she's doing (not just the image of the activity) and has relationships with her instructors and peers.

Extracurricular activities open new worlds of sports, culture, and leisure to children. Each activity has unique benefits and unique challenges. The entitlement child expects the world to do things *her way*. The entitlement-free child steps out into a world of opportunities to see what she might enjoy and what she might learn. Some choices will be a clear fit with your child and your family. Others will be hit-and-miss. Each choice helps your child learn something new about herself and the world around her.

FOLLOW THE CROWD

Situation: My child hates gymnastics but wants to sign up because all her friends will be there.

Entitlement Issues: The entitlement child tries to do it all and have it all. You want your child to have all the same opportunities as her peers. Just because she doesn't like gymnastics doesn't mean she can't make something out of it. Most importantly, you want your child to be well-liked and accepted. If your child starts following her own interests, her "old friends" will start to exclude her from other activities too.

Entitlement-Free Perspective: Deciding the best use of your child's time is an individual decision. Everyone can't have everything, so the entitlement-free child learns to weigh compromises. Joining an activity to be with friends and then acting disruptive or disinterested is not entitlement-free. Joining an activity to be with your friends and agreeing to make a full commitment, even though it isn't your favorite activity, is entitlement-free.

Similarly, overloading your child's schedule so she doesn't miss anything leads to entitlement burnout. Teach your child the consequences of one choice over another, which leads to entitlement-free responsibility. Can your child give up something she likes in order to be with her friends? Can she register for a short period of time to find out if it's worth giving up something else? The entitlement-free child learns to make decisions and abide by her decisions in a can't-have-it-all world.

ENTITLEMENT-FREE STRATEGIES

1. **Decide a reasonable number of activities that your child and your household can sustain.** Consider time and finances, as well as your child's need for non-entertainment and slow time (for daydreaming and "doing nothing"). In most cases, one or two simultaneous activities are plenty. Choose a number that allows you leeway for short-term opportunities like summer swimming lessons or a holiday with grandparents.

2. **Discuss with your child the minimal level of commitment expected:** showing up on time even when you don't feel like it, staying focused even when you aren't good at something, showing support for friends who are enjoying themselves, and agreeing to attend a minimum number of classes before dropping out. Age-appropriate expectations give your child the opportunity to learn from mistakes. Either design shorter commitments for younger children or opt to wait until the level of commitment matches your child's ability.

3. **Give your child time to make a realistic decision about joining an activity.** Children aren't always capable of predicting future feelings. If your child wants something now, she believes she'll want it tomorrow as well. Take a week or two to explain the choices to your child in a few different ways. Try a reality check like, "If you were going to gymnastics today, you couldn't ride your bike after school," or "It's fun to play with your friends at school, but you know you won't be able to act silly together during gymnastics."

4. Enforce the expectations of the agreement. Your child learns the power of decision making by living with the consequences of her choices. If you regret taking an activity, try to stand by a reasonable commitment. If you regret not taking an activity, focus on what you and your child will do differently next time.

QUITTING

Situation: My child has asked to quit the last four activities he joined, and I don't know if I should let him quit this time.

Entitlement Issues: Children are not "quitters." That's a ridiculous label that's left over from a time when parents bullied children into adult-like behavior. Why waste time doing things you don't want to do? Childhood is a time to try new things in order to discover what you like and don't like. The sooner you eliminate things you don't like, the sooner you find the things you do like.

Sometimes good intentions create a negative entitlement pattern. The entitlement child, unable to see the big picture, learns to act impulsively. Over time, this child doesn't know the difference between trying and not trying, or he forms opinions before giving something a chance.

Entitlement-Free Perspective: Children don't always know best, especially in emotionally loaded situations. Your child might be overwhelmed, struggling with excessive demands, or he might have a fear of failure and need encouragement instead of an easy out. The entitlement-free child learns to look at difficult situations with your guidance instead of reacting impulsively. He learns to build on his strengths and to face age-appropriate difficulties, like the need for additional practice or being the new kid in the group. As in most parenting situations, strive for balance. Making a habit of quitting is a red flag, but never quitting can be a warning sign too. Changing instructors once might be productive, but all instructors can't be the problem.

ENTITLEMENT-FREE STRATEGIES

1. **Give yourself time to listen to and observe your child.** Why might he think he wants to quit? Does he complain when going to class but is happy at the end of class? Is he happy until performance time? What else might be happening? Are there minor friendship squabbles or temporary disappointments?

2. **Look for common reasons behind quitting multiple activities.** Your child may be giving up too soon, when expectations rise or additional focus is required. Or it's possible that the activities have been a mismatch. Perhaps they were group dominated, sports-themed, or at a stressful time of day. If so, the pattern may not be your child's behavior but poor planning that can be adjusted next time.

3. **Refrain from using hurtful labels like "quitter."** Labels undermine constructive action. Parent your child as an individual, and stay away from parenting absolutes like "always" and "never."

4. **To offset impulsivity, establish standards to live by.** Did your child give his best effort? Did he give this enough time? Did he fulfill his commitment to the other people affected by his decision? The entitlement-free child understands that his decisions affect other people.

5. **Help your child work on specific problems and practice basic skills in familiar settings, like your living room or backyard.** Help your child prepare for situations that confuse him in class, like a surprise demonstration or abrupt directions. Rehearse social skills to prepare for group personalities such as the joker, the best player, or the "queen bee."

6. **Choose activities that match your child's personality and current abilities.** An active child may have great difficulty sitting for piano lessons this year but would do fine with another instrument or waiting for another time. Some children prefer solitary activities to team sports. Find activities that complement your child's social, emotional, intellectual, and physical abilities. Your child may even enjoy learning new skills when he's not the best. Either way, choose activities based on input from the entitlement-free child.

THE UNDESERVED NO

Situation: My child wants a horse, but I'm not sure we have the time or the resources for such an expensive activity.

Entitlement Issues: To sacrifice or not to sacrifice—that is the question. You want to give your child everything she wants, especially if you believe she's "earned it." She loves horses, knows everything there is to know about horses, and genuinely agrees to care for the horse. How can you not make this a family priority? The entitlement parent puts the child's interest and desire above everything else, including money, time, or other family priorities.

Entitlement-Free Perspective: Just because you want to make your child's dreams come true doesn't mean you should. This is a family decision that requires honest deliberation over the impact on the family for years to come. A horse is a bigger commitment than a goldfish, and much bigger than a puppy. The entitlement child never knows the personal sacrifice that others make in order to grant her wishes, believing instead that all dreams magically come true. The entitlement-free child understands the difference between a privilege and a right. Owning a horse is a privilege.

ENTITLEMENT-FREE STRATEGIES

1. **Consider the length and breadth of your child's commitment to owning a horse.** You want to be reasonably certain that your child's interest is ongoing and long-term. Riding lessons and horse care should be well-established habits that fit into everyone's schedule before any further discussion.

2. **Have a family meeting to outline the financial and logistical requirements.** Discuss who will be responsible for feeding and exercising the horse when your child is busy, consider all of the related costs, and make sure this a commitment everyone is willing to make. If not, stop the discussion there. Let your child know this is a choice the family cannot make at this time…sorry.

3. **Encourage your child to follow her passion to the level that works for the family at this time.** Suggest books and imaginative activities, volunteer work at a local stable, or regular riding lessons. Saying no does not prevent your child from learning as much as she can now.

4. If a horse is in your child's future, enlist your child in the care of the horse as well as the pleasure of having a horse. Caring for an animal is not a sometimes, when-I feel-like-it proposition. It is an all-the-time commitment that teaches the entitlement-free child the give and take of a reciprocal relationship.

EQUAL TIME

Situation: The coach doesn't give my child equal playing time.

Entitlement Issues: Children's activities should be about playing, not about competing with peers, watching from the sidelines, or being the best. Whether the activity is sports, music, or dance, children should receive equal attention, regardless of talent or ability. The entitlement child signs up for fun and is upset to discover that achievement is rewarded.

Entitlement-Free Perspective: There are many reasons to participate in an activity. Some activities are social and fun-oriented, while others are more performance-based. You can choose the kind of activity that fits your child's needs, but you must also realize that other people may prefer something different. If you choose to enroll your child in a performance-based group, be sure your child cares about the particular activity. Each player only gets to bat a few times in a T-ball game, infielders have more to do than outfielders, and the child with the loudest voice gets center stage.

If your child is not interested in the specific skills of an activity, let him happily be part of the ensemble. Make choices that fit your child. He may be thrilled to see his friend in the spotlight, or he may be ecstatic when getting dressed for dance class and prefer to perform for you at home later. Above all, consider whether the activity is good for your child, not whether someone else is getting something more.

ENTITLEMENT-FREE STRATEGIES

1. **Be careful about comparisons.** Your child may not share your concerns. If your child is happy playing while you are cataloguing inequities, stop worrying. Enjoy the moment. There'll be time later to intervene when your child asks for your help.

2. **Follow your child's lead.** When your child becomes curious about improving his performance, it's time to reevaluate his commitment to the activity. Is he ready to learn more and do more? Discuss what's involved with achieving his goals, such as more practice or time away from something else he enjoys. If he wants to try, make a plan together. Practice at home, watch how the professionals do it, and talk to the coach about your child's interest.

3. **Talk about unfairness in age-appropriate ways.** Sometimes grown-ups have favorites (and while you wish that were never true, it is). The entitlement-free child learns as much from how you handle the personal dynamics as from the activity itself. Explain to your child that you understand that it doesn't feel good when someone is singled out in a group for attention. Try to think together of other ways to make the activity fun.

WINNERS AND LOSERS

Situation: My child participated in an activity but did not receive an award. Awards should be given to everyone for participating in an activity, not based on winners and losers.

Entitlement Issues: All children are winners. You want your child to be successful and to feel positive about all she can do. Entitlement children deserve situations that boost their self-esteem and make them feel good about themselves. There's plenty of time later for the real world of competition and hard knocks.

Entitlement-Free Perspective: Teach your child the intrinsic value of experiences regardless of the outcome. Time is well spent in an activity because you want to be there. You have fun, you learn something new, you want to be with other people, and you've worked hard preparing to do your best. Introducing prizes and rewards changes the deal, placing the focus on the external value of the experience (performance, speed, time, distance, points, or score). The entitlement-free child approaches prizes and rewards as part of the game, not a reflection of individual worth.

Entitlement-free children, because they learn to see events from another's point of view, become more graceful losers. They may not like it at first, but they know how to live with sadness, disappointment, jealousy, or impatience. It's not okay to stomp away when your friend wins something you want, or to say mean things to other children because they won and you didn't.

ENTITLEMENT-FREE STRATEGIES

1. **Talk about winning and losing in games or events.** Help your child to comprehend the rules: "Can everyone win this game? What would that look like?" Laugh about the silliness of everyone crossing the finish line together or all teams getting the same score every time. Prepare your child for competitive games by talking about the

difference between games where everyone wins and ones where someone loses. All winners lose sometime.

2. **Build frustration "muscles."** Practice with small, private losses at board games or backyard races before exposing your child to public losses. Should you let your entitlement-free child win? Probably, once in a while you should. Winning teaches your child to strive for something, just as losing teaches your child that she still has something to learn. It's a thoughtful balance: you increase challenges as your child's skills increase. Eventually, she will learn to win independent of your generosity.

3. **Teach disappointment strategies.** Acknowledge that it doesn't feel good to lose. Say, "You don't like losing." Practice letting it go. Communicate to your child that once the game is over, you can't change what happened, but you can change next time. Plan together what your child can do differently.

4. **Focus on a different point of view, and engage your child in hypothetical thinking.** Ask, "What would it feel like to be the winner?" or "What would you do with a trophy if you won?" Ask your child if she thinks other children are sad about not winning, or to consider what the losing team should do now.

ANTICIPATING FAILURE

Situation: My child wants to go to surf camp but is afraid of sea creatures. I think he'll want to come home when he gets there. I don't want to throw the money away when I know it isn't going to work out.

Entitlement Issues: The entitlement child wants what he wants and promises anything to get it. He is also free to change his mind without regard for cost or commitment.

Entitlement-Free Perspective: Parents help entitlement-free children understand the expectations of a new venture. They help children fill in the gaps between what they know and what they don't know—surfer kids are cool, but they also get saltwater in their faces and minnows nibbling on their toes.

Give your child the responsibility of choice. If he wants to sign up for camp, he can't change his mind mid-summer and start something else. The entitlement-free child makes the choice, but it is the guiding parent who helps him understand the decision he's making. The parent also carries the ultimate veto power.

ENTITLEMENT-FREE STRATEGIES

1. **First, find out why your child wants to attend this program, keeping in mind that children are very bad at answering "why" questions.** Is he curious about ocean life in books and videos, or is he identifying with a fictitious Nemo? Genuine curiosity is relevant, but fantasy-only suggests that your child may need more maturity before tackling the real situation.

2. **Take your child to the ocean while you explain the conditions of the actual class.** Children who really want to learn something new may feel ready to conquer mild fears for short periods of time. Watch your child's reactions in class-like situations. Is your child's motivation stronger in comparable situations, or is it

questionable? There's no shame in not being ready this year if your child is hesitant.

3. **Explain the commitment of camp to your child.** Registering for camp is more than a day at the beach. It's a decision about where you want to spend a lot of time. Choosing surf camp means not choosing theater camp. Show your child *how* to make decisions by looking at the pros and cons together.

4. **Only make the decision if *you* confidently believe it's the right decision and if you are prepared to stand by the decision.** For example, if your child has an intense fear of the water after the first week, consider that you will likely regret the decision and have to live with a cranky child for the rest of the summer. You always have the parental prerogative to postpone surf camp until next year, when your child has more skills and adaptability.

SKIPPING CLASS

Situation: My child doesn't want to go to dance class today because her best friend is away on vacation.

Entitlement Issues: Friends sign up for classes together to enjoy a shared activity. There's no point in forcing your child to do something she doesn't want to do. She isn't going to participate if she doesn't want to be there. And the time can be much better spent doing something she likes.

Entitlement-Free Perspective: Flexibility is a sign of an entitlement-free child. You don't have to insist on 100 percent attendance (though that might be a worthwhile goal), but your child may discover new reasons to enjoy a class. Encourage your child to explore "what if": What if her friend is away? Will she find someone else to talk to? Will she feel the same or feel awkward? Will she be surprised by how much she knows?

Because children by nature are entitlement thinkers, they often lack the adult logical ability to imagine future events. But with your help, the entitlement-free child experiences success by taking chances on things she thought she didn't want to do. The secret is to give her the skills to handle the new experiences.

ENTITLEMENT-FREE STRATEGIES

1. **Listen to your child's reservations, and help her articulate difficult emotions like fear or self-consciousness.** Empathize with your child's feelings. Assure her that it's normal to be nervous the first time you do something alone. Tell her, "Of course you'd like your friend with you, because you know how much she likes going to dance class."

2. **Think of behaviors to manage the difficult feelings.** Remind your child that the sequence of the class is the same even if her friend isn't there: put her backpack in the cubby, say hello to the teacher, do some stretching, and practice the new dance routine. ("You can do it!") Ask if your child would like you to walk in with her or wait at the door when class is over. Introduce baby steps to independence that will make the first time a little easier.

3. **Brainstorm other points of view.** Remind your child that the other children want to see her even when her friend is away, and the instructor will miss her if she doesn't go. Ask, "Won't it be fun to be able to teach your friend the dance moves when she comes back?"

4. Build confidence through experience. Every time your child does something she didn't know she could do, she increases her repertoire for the future. Take every advantage of opportunities to do something new.

BAIT-AND-SWITCH

Situation: Karate was all fun and games last year. Now the expectations are higher, and my child is struggling.

Entitlement Issues: This feels like a bait-and-switch and is not fair to children at all. Children need consistency. Rules and expectations shouldn't change. You want your child to continue to attend classes, because this has been a familiar and happy place in his life for a long time. Now, he doesn't understand why there's new attention to performance and details.

Entitlement-Free Perspective: Expectations for the entitlement-free child change as he grows. This is particularly true in skill-oriented activities where mastery and maturity increase from year to year. At some point, depending on the age of the children or the particular philosophy of the instructor, the particular sport or craft starts to be emphasized over the more general social aspects of the activity. Your child may have liked the activity when it was simply fun, but at this new level, it's no longer a good fit.

Help your child learn to evaluate his options and make choices that fit his needs and those of his family. Adapting to a changing world is essential to entitlement-free thinking, as is the awareness that different programs meet different needs. Only the entitlement child believes that everyone else's needs are the same as his needs.

There is a difference between debilitating frustration and the short-term frustration of trying something new. Encourage your child through temporary setbacks, and he'll acquire confidence by managing difficulty—not being insulated from it.

Entitlement-Free Strategies

1. **Be informed.** Expect programs to change periodically; otherwise the activity is not growing with the children. If your child attends an activity that has an adult version (sports, dance, some music programs), ask about when it gets "serious" and how the program introduces the profession to the children.

2. **Monitor activities to ensure they are developmentally appropriate for your child.** There's a difference between appropriate directions like "Let me see you focus like a black belt," and inappropriate directions like "This isn't just fun anymore, so toughen up." Young children are not equipped to manage abuse or humiliation. You can, however, help your child understand new expectations that stretch skills in appropriate ways. For example, "Show me the difference between karate-class sparring and silly-pretend sparring—I want to see your control."

3. **Make effort fun and a means to an end.** Introduce your child to people and peers who have reached the next level in an activity. Take your child to watch practices as well as big events.

4. **Help your child respond to increased demands.** Make sure that not everything in your child's schedule is high pressure (school, sports, and family). Add listening time

and down time. Show your child concrete ways he "can do it." (Praise alone won't do it.) For example, if you want to help your child focus on his body, you can observe how children stand in karate class versus how the children stand in line at school.

5. **Revisit choices regularly.** Unless your child is a prodigy in a particular activity and innately driven to perfect specific skills and talents, commit to only a few sessions at a time. Routinely compare other options as you see new interests emerging in your child.

Extracurricular activities offer you and your child wonderful opportunities to play, to learn, and to grow. They expose children to new roles and new rules—different programs, different instructors, and peers with different abilities. Go slowly. The entitlement-free child doesn't need to do everything and learn everything *right now.* Choose the activities that match your child's temperament and personal strengths. Consider how extracurricular activities fit into your child's school day and home life. Entitlement-free parenting is purposeful and selective.

Make choices that truly benefit your child. Define "enough," and understand what your child enjoys, as well as what sustains her interest and curiosity. Choose activities that your child cares about. Caring creates commitment. Consider whether a particular commitment works for your child and your family at a given time. All children do not need all activities. It's better to do one or two things respectfully than many things carelessly.

10

MONEY AND GIFTS

ENTITLEMENT-FREE PRINCIPLES

- **Teach practical and ethical money skills.**
- **Teach your child how to respectfully care for property and possessions.**
- **Feel the power of "no," "not yet," and "enough."**

Using money always involves problem solving. The amount of money you have is always less than the number of ways you have to spend it. Spending money is a choice. (This or that? Now or later? For me or for someone else?) The entitlement-free child is taught about money in order to learn responsible decision making and to gain independent skills. Learning about money is an ongoing process corresponding to changing developmental abilities.

Money is an abstract concept for young children, involving specific mathematical properties (e.g., one five-dollar bill buys more than ten quarters) and countless ideological assumptions (e.g., money is difficult to acquire or money is easily available; money buys happiness, respect, love; money can help people). The entitlement-free child learns the nuances of money: what it is, where it comes from, how to earn it, and how to spend it.

He also acquires critical ideas about money long before he's old enough to understand the mechanics of numeracy or commerce. Allowances, play-money, giving and receiving gifts—all shape hands-on learning and the idea that some things are more precious than others. Everyday situations teach the entitlement-free child about mine-and-yours ownership as well as the generosity of giving and taking.

Young children think magically. Of course money could grow on trees—why not? Bank machines might be friendly robots that spew out free dollar bills. No amount of reason will eradicate the benign fairies in children's imaginations. But forward-looking adults can include helpful routines and rituals that teach children value and responsibility. Never mind that a jar of colorful beach glass is more valuable to your child than an expensive piece of jewelry. To a child, a stack of pennies can be a greater treasure than a five-dollar bill. Value is age-specific.

The adult extravagances of entitlement are not good for children. Childhood riches are found elsewhere, in loving and being loved. The entitlement-free child develops an appreciation for people, things, and experiences; and as a result, he always has "enough." Your child learns "enough" when he takes that giant step from Me-Mine-Now to respect and responsibility.

Establish a foundation for entitlement-free living by helping your child choose carefully what he wants, take care of the things he values, appreciate what others give without entitlement, and learn to give as well as receive. Ownership, like sharing, is a complex concept for children. It may take half a lifetime for a child to understand the boundaries between yours and mine. (Teenagers are classically confused on this subject.) With an entitlement-free foundation, you won't have to undo years of overindulgence.

BORROWED AND BROKEN

Situation: A friend forgot a well-worn toy at our house. When my child played with it, he broke it.

Entitlement Issues: The entitlement response can come from two different directions. One, it's not the child's fault: he handled the toy appropriately and did not break it on purpose. Or two: the parent accepts full responsibility and rushes out to replace the toy for the child. Either way, entitlement thinking takes the child out of the equation.

Entitlement-Free Perspective: Children are not born knowing what responsible action looks like. They learn it by rules and example. Learning to do the right thing starts with an awareness of how your child's actions make a difference to other people. Honesty when no one is looking and thoughtfulness in accidental situations are necessary on these harmless occasions if they are to be encouraged in riskier situations. The entitlement-free child steps up.

Situations like this one are character-building opportunities for your child, setting a precedent for caring for another person's things when they are in your possession. Years from now, this may be the difference between caring about the owner of a lost wallet and stepping over someone else's problem.

ENTITLEMENT-FREE STRATEGIES

1. **Discuss the situation with your child from the other child's point of view.** Talk about the fact that when

people leave or lose things at someone else's house, they hope that that person (especially if he's a friend) will be kind and considerate and watch over the item as if it were his own.

2. **Help your child admit his role in the situation.** The entitlement-free child initiates the phone call or brings the broken toy back to his friend. He offers remedies— to pay for the toy, to offer one of his own as a replacement, or to buy a new one. Taking responsibility requires honesty.

3. **Include your child in the solution.** The entitlement-free child is vested in the solution by using his money, contributing to the cost, or by "earning" a portion of the payment. Your child's contribution need not be financial; he could make amends by doing something nice. Entitlement-free responsibility teaches your child that everyone plays a part in making things right in the world.

ALLOWANCES

Situation: My child wants the same allowance her friend gets, but I don't see why a child needs so much money when the parents buy everything she needs.

Entitlement Issues: This is a new era. Children expect to have their own cash to buy things they like. It isn't fair that one child can buy anything she likes and your child is left out of the fun. Besides, if your child has money of her own, she won't be nagging and whining, asking you to buy her things.

Entitlement-Free Perspective: The entitlement child is still spending your money, whether it's in your pocket or hers.

Allowances are not about who's holding the cash but about the responsibility that comes with holding the cash. The entitlement-free child receives an allowance to learn how to manage money, not to boost her buying potential. Your child's allowance is an age-appropriate game to learn independence and decision making.

A good practice is to divide allowance money between needs, wants, saving, and giving. For the most part, parents pay for a child's needs, but you could include a regular "need" like snack money or a subway token. (Even if the child is too young to do these things alone, she might still carry her "own" money.) Wants might be prizes at the dollar store or money for additions to a toy-car collection. Savings might be for Dad's birthday gift or for a special toy. And giving could be for the church basket, weekly tzedakah, or pennies for charity. The entitlement-free child is given options and limits that steer her to great decisions.

Entitlement-Free Strategies

1. **Decide the goal of allowances in advance.** This establishes the rules of the game, to ensure that you're teaching what you intend to teach. What do you think is appropriate for you to buy, versus what your child is permitted to buy without your consent, if anything? Teach your child the joy of paying for a surprise toy or planning ahead for a special gift for someone special. Start with the kinds of choices your child is ready to make, and build from there.

2. **Decide how much money to give your child.** The amount of the allowance should be determined by your child's maturity to take responsibility for purchases. An

allowance is not a blank check (or an open debit card). If you're encouraging your child to buy expensive toys, these are things that you are not buying. If your child is using her money to buy birthday gifts for her friends, you will want to monitor the situation so that the money will be there when she needs it. Start simple. Even before your child understands the math, you can show her three items that she can afford and one that she cannot.

3. **Money is power.** Give your child a little at a time. Your child doesn't need to be burdened by expenditures and investment strategies, but she can experience what money does and does not do. Having money in a piggy bank or in a pocket prompts understanding and decision making.

4. **Keep your financial lessons casual and age-appropriate.** Your child is your apprentice, shadowing you in your adult world. Clue her in to things you take for granted. She will enjoy the game and learn much more.

MONEY FOR CHORES

Situation: Now that my child is starting to understand the negotiation power of money, he's always looking for ways to earn more. I can't get him to do anything without "paying" him.

Entitlement Issues: Industriousness can't possibly be connected to entitlement. Your child is showing eagerness, helpfulness, and ingenuity. Besides, you'd give him the money one way or another anyway; why not get a little something back for it?

Entitlement-Free Perspective: Who's really in charge? If your child has shrewdly orchestrated a chance to get his way, if he's pushing the limits of more-more-more, if you feel a little smirk behind your back and sense your child is thinking, "Gotcha," it's time to rethink the arrangement. The entitlement-free child knows that everyone in the family helps in the household without always being paid. It's what families do; they care for each other. Labors of love are required of the entitlement-free child.

ENTITLEMENT-FREE STRATEGIES

1. **Distinguish between allowance and non-paying chores.** Teach your child that everyone in the family does certain things for the family without pay. That's not to say everyone's labor isn't greatly appreciated and acknowledged—Dad's cooking, Mom's grocery shopping, walking the dog, or cleaning the ring around the bathtub are all appreciated.

2. **Encourage your child to help around the house without pay, starting at a young age.**

TWO-YEAR-OLDS

- Dusting (with feather dusters)
- Throwing dirty laundry into the hamper
- Putting toys on toy shelves or sorting into bins
- Tossing salads or stirring ingredients
- Buttering bread or adding jelly
- Wiping tables or plastic placemats
- Sweeping the patio

- Pulling a wagon with recycling bins to the curb (supervised, of course)
- Watering gardens
- Washing plastic riding toys

THREE-YEAR-OLDS: ALL OF THE ABOVE, PLUS...

- Cleaning sliding doors and mirrors (with spray bottles)
- Emptying the dryer (supervised, of course)
- Sorting socks or taking baskets of clothes to family members' rooms
- Setting the table
- Scooping cold cereal and pouring milk from child-size containers
- Feeding the dog or the fish
- Hosing down the sidewalk after sidewalk chalk drawing
- Picking up litter
- Vacuuming the car mats with a hand vacuum
- Planting herbs and flowers

FOUR- AND FIVE-YEAR-OLDS: ALL OF THE ABOVE, PLUS...

- Folding laundry
- Putting clothes in drawers
- Clearing the table
- Washing and drying plastic dishes
- Washing fruits and vegetables
- Emptying the dishwasher (supervised, after knives are removed)
- Peeling potatoes and carrots

- Bringing in the mail, sorting envelopes from magazines, sorting by name
- Washing the car (with a grown-up, of course)
- Weeding the garden

Older children can do all of the above plus help adults with their activities.

3. **Say no or redirect the situation when your child tests his entrepreneurship on you.** Smile and say, "Nice try." Remind your child of how your family works: helping and working together are not optional. If you want to encourage your child's fiscal ingenuity, help him make a "business plan" to offer a helpful service to the neighbors. Also include a plan for the money earned.

SPENDING SPREES

Situation: When my child receives birthday money from her grandparents, she'll spend it as fast as she can on the first things she sees. She won't stop her shopping spree until every cent is spent.

Entitlement Issues: You want your child to make independent choices. It's her money, after all. She should be the one to spend it. Eventually, she'll understand how much money she wasted on things she didn't need.

Entitlement-Free Perspective: The free-spender feels the adrenaline of entitlement: buy now and buy more. What fun is thinking, planning, or waiting when your child is in the middle of a spending frenzy? Natural consequences won't work here, because the entitlement child doesn't care about the consequences. So what if you spend all your money on junk? Spending sprees aren't about appreciating what you buy; they're about the immediate pleasure of buying, regardless of *what* you buy. The entitlement-free child has limits to guide her actions when she isn't able to show restraint.

ENTITLEMENT-FREE STRATEGIES

1. **Teach your child how to prioritize.** Ask her to make a list of ten things she wants to buy (or cut pictures from catalogs or websites) and sequence them according to which to buy first. Check back weekly to add new items or delete old ones. This exercise alone will demonstrate how wants can change from one day to the next.

2. **Take a list, or at least have a plan, before going shopping with your child.** Your child isn't rational once the shopping frenzy begins. Decide, in advance, if this trip to the mall is to buy something. If so, be specific about what it is; if not, enjoy window shopping. With clear expectations, it will be easier to stay focused.

3. **Make window shopping a stress-free alternative to spending sprees.** Invent your own non-buying shopping rituals that make not buying as much fun as buying. Set a shopping challenge: who can spend the least amount over one dollar? Play a shopping scavenger hunt: find polka-dot socks, the ugliest tie ever made, and twins wearing the same outfit. Guess the price: is it worth it? Play "money what-if": If you could buy any one thing in the store, what would you buy, and why? Or what if you had one hundred dollars to buy the only toys a child would ever have? What would you buy, and why? This is great for other purchasing choices too: If you had five dollars to buy five days of

snacks, what would you buy? Or what if you only had one thousand dollars to live on? Where could you live for one year?

4. **Enforce a predetermined limit on all shopping adventures.** Set the amount based on your personal budget or the spending portion of your child's allowance, or be creative (two-dollar Tuesdays, cheapskate Saturdays, or it-took-me-three-months-to-save-for-this-day-and-I-finally-did-it). Self-control begins with external boundaries. Once your child can operate within the boundaries, she may be ready to make more independent choices. Until then, feel free to exercise your veto power.

EXTRAVAGANT BIRTHDAY PARTIES

Situation: My child is expecting an awesome birthday this year. Every time he comes home from someone else's party, he says he can't wait for his party, because it'll be the best of all. His friends have had the best of everything; I can't imagine what else I can do. The pressure is intense.

Entitlement Issues: Birthday parties are special times. You don't want to disappoint your child, so you accept this as one of the responsibilities of parenthood and give it your best. If it means losing a little sleep or spending a little extra, your child is worth it.

Entitlement-Free Perspective: Sometimes, when exuberance and excitement are high, children get confused about what makes them happy. They want bigger, better, and more. Bigger what? Better how? More what? This unnamed desire is insatiable.

Birthday party "consumers" are always looking for the next party idea, the most innovative party theme, or the first one to book a new venue. The parent who tries to win this game will never do enough or give enough. They just set the bar higher for the next person. The entitlement-free child needs you to plan a party that reflects *his* heart's desire—not get fooled by a retailer's sales pitch or keep up with the Joneses.

ENTITLEMENT-FREE STRATEGIES

1. **Know your limits.** The definition of a "good parent" does not include spending more than you have or buying more in order to keep up with others. The entitlement-free child is, by now, so familiar with the concept of limits that he won't be shocked to hear there's a limit on what you plan to spend or on the number of children invited. (Feel free to sing "Happy Birthday" a million and one times.)

2. **Customize your child's birthday celebration to reflect what *he* likes.** Collect information after your child attends other parties: what did he like, not like, or want to repeat? Take a chance and let your child "design" the event. Your child may prefer watermelon with chocolate sprinkles instead of a birthday cake—try it. Help your child know his heart, whether he likes inside activities or outside, water balloons or helium, silly sequins or traditional attire. You may need to say that live elephants are not allowed at the real party but the elephants can certainly attend his "imaginary party." You can also opt for a tried-and-true party location like the local pavilion or your child's favorite and familiar gym. Just remember to align your expectations with your child's point of view.

3. **No excuses are necessary for being different.** If your party is child-centered with child-sized fun, let guests know what to expect. Tell them on invitations how to dress for this particular fun-making, and tell them about any birthday-rule breaking, so your guests will be ready for the unexpected.

4. **Failure is not an option with friends.** Create a guest list of people that you and your child like and who like you. Children's birthday parties are not mandatory business obligations. The focus of the party should remain on celebrating with childlike abandon, not looking over your shoulder for critical disdain. You want your child to believe that the people who come to his party are coming because they are his friends or yours.

EXTRAVAGANT BIRTHDAY GIFTS

Situation: I can't believe the expensive gifts my child receives from children we barely know. I cannot afford to reciprocate with a comparable gift, especially when we are invited to multiple parties every weekend.

Entitlement Issues: Birthday party etiquette is an emotionally charged, social game of who gets invited to parties and who is accepted in certain groups. Isn't there a "rule" that an expensive party requires an expensive gift, equal to the per-guest cost of the party? If you want your child to be included, this is the price of friendship.

Entitlement-Free Perspective: Affordability is not the issue; restraint is. The entitlement child has too much, too soon. Children have a hard enough time understanding age-appropriate limits without being showered in excessive 'ement children fed with silver spoons ⸺ne norm for everyone. They learn to expect ⸺ without appreciating the essential values of grat-⸺de and friendship. Boutique clothes and designer toys become the measure of friendship instead of the qualities of a true friend.

The entitlement-free child learns that relationships are more important than presents. There is a connection between giving and receiving; gift buying teaches the entitlement-free child about friendship. Help your child to consider whether gift buying is an attempt to do something nice for someone else or just another inconvenient dash to the mall. Children may be better off without party presents rather than witnessing stressed-out, resentful grown-ups fulfilling superficial obligations.

ENTITLEMENT-FREE STRATEGIES

1. **Give birthdays back to the children—the sooner, the better.** Understand that entitlement children are immersed in consumerism at a young age. They get bored quickly and can get temporarily disoriented without media markers. Get your child involved in planning a wonderful birthday gift: think of what the birthday child likes, what the birthday child already has, what will make her laugh, what the birthday child hasn't done yet, and what your child can share with her.

2. **Dare to be original.** Think outside the box. What would the birthday child really like? Maybe it's a Home Depot apron, goggles, and a basket of wood pieces (glue and paint optional), or a beautiful teacup with cookie cutters and batter. Be careful not to lose perspective. Gifts are

still about pleasing the other person, not "educating" them. (Not everyone appreciates homemade gifts or donations made in their child's name.)

3. **Offer to make a birthday pact with your child's close friends or play-group circle.** Everyone might be relieved to have some celebration ground rules. Of course, there are always people who stretch the limits—chalk it up to human nature. You can, however, openly discuss the stresses and insanity of birthday excess.

4. **Consider a present-free party.** Ask guests to include a note in the birthday card listing favorite books, videos, jokes, or places to visit. Or on the invitation, state your preference for books-only gifts or wrapped toys for charity.

GRATITUDE

Situation: The grandparents always buy my child extravagant gifts that are completely inappropriate at this age. My child is sad and disappointed when he opens them.

Entitlement Issues: You expect adults to know better, especially if you've given them a few helpful suggestions. You don't blame your child for expressing his disappointment, and you hope that the grandparents will get the picture eventually. You feel so bad that your child has been cheated out of a nice present that you take him to the store for a replacement gift.

Entitlement-Free Perspective: Children are naturally focused on themselves, but the entitlement-free child learns to be gracious, kind, and considerate even when disappointed. He learns that all gifts are an act of generosity, and to express gratitude despite disappointment. Disappointment is more manageable for the entitlement-free child, because he grows in an atmosphere of "enough." He has enough, so he doesn't need one more perfect thing to feel completely satisfied. He is loved enough, so people aren't desperately trying to reassure him. This foundation allows him to notice acts of goodwill from another person's point of view.

Over time, the entitlement-free child learns to appreciate the idiosyncrasies, and sometimes peculiarities, of other people without feeling personally betrayed. He may not understand today why Grandma thinks those stock options are interesting to a little boy, or why Grandpa keeps buying those Tiffany cuff links when his shirts have buttonholes. But he can appreciate the gift anyway, and he may be pleasantly surprised to discover that today's gift will be valued or valuable twenty years from now.

ENTITLEMENT-FREE STRATEGIES

1. **Teach your child to appreciate the giving as much as the gift.** This starts with learning to say "thank you" and grows with your child's increasing age and ability to acknowledge the gesture as well as the particular gift. Teach your child simple truisms like "All gifts are special," or "Sometimes it takes a long time to know what makes each gift special."

2. **Prepare your child for the unexpected.** It's easy for children to expect the toy-of-the-year or the perfect pony. Talk about wishing and hoping and the possibility of surprises. If you suspect an upcoming gift mismatch, discuss different possible reactions instead of leaving your child unprepared in an emotional moment. Be clear about your expectations: "If you don't like Grandma's present,

you can tell me in the car. But be sure to say 'thank you,' and do not throw the present in the corner."

3. **Do what you can to help your child understand the gift-giver's point of view.** Children do not automatically see the world through other people's eyes. They need your help. You don't have to lie or conjure up good intentions; neutral descriptions are sufficient. For example, "Grandma thought you'd like it. She didn't get it right, did she?" Or, "Grandpa thinks you like what he likes. At least he remembered you." Or, "Sometimes people don't know what children like."

4. **Do not buy substitute presents.** Gifts are between the giver and the receiver. Look at all the ways you give your child enough. Teach your child all the ways the gift-giver is a valuable person even if they never get gift-giving right.

5. **Give the gift-giver opportunities to learn more about your child and his interests throughout the year.** Sometimes improving the relationship can create greater understanding between that person and your child. A superficial gift is sometimes a substitute for a meaningful relationship.

HOLIDAY GIMMES

Situation: My child is obsessed with holiday presents. She oohs and ahs at mountains of presents and feels sorry for children who only get one or two things. I don't want to be a Scrooge, but how much is too much?

Entitlement Issues: Holidays are for children. You want to make them as special as possible and create lasting memories.

Entitlement-Free Perspective: The visual effect of a mountain of presents certainly is dramatic, filled with the excitement of surprises and wishes fulfilled. Holiday magic also twinkles in Christmas lights and Chanukah candles. It's captured in the images of Santa's workshop and gingerbread houses with candy-cane chimneys. The entitlement-free child is mesmerized by joyful celebrations. Holidays are a time to celebrate religious or secular events with family and friends; they are so much more than just gift-giving.

ENTITLEMENT-FREE STRATEGIES

1. **Choose holiday traditions, in addition to gift-giving, that reflect your beliefs.** Whether it's caroling or wearing your pajamas in the car to look at decorated house lights, collecting toys for homeless children or making cards for seniors in the assisted living center, there are plenty of enjoyable holiday activities the family can do together in addition to giving presents. Include other child-oriented activities: baking cookies, decorating the house, or lighting pretend chanukiahs or opening Advent calendars. The gifts won't be "too much" when other holiday experiences are "just right."

2. **Teach your child to ask for what she wants but not to expect everything.** Decide on what's enough, based on what feels right to you. Just be sure there is a limit. (No, you don't have to go into withdrawal the first year.) Have your child ask Santa for two presents or ten, knowing that Santa can't bring everything you wish for. Open presents one night of Chanukah or give eight little presents, such as pairs of socks and dollar-store finds. Your child will

appreciate tradition as you define it in your home, because it's hers and hers alone.

3. **Give suggestions to family and friends to help curb gift overload.** Remember to communicate your preferences without demanding compliance. Some people will welcome your recommendations, while others will still obstinately buy the weird singing elf with the scary ears.

4. **Say no to the things you can control.** Explain to your child that some things are out of the question. This is an opportunity to explain the concept of value, and not just make Santa the bad guy who doesn't bring the present. Say no to the junk toys that aren't worth the money and to the inappropriate toys that your child can't have for a few more years (or never). A well-timed no gives the entitlement-free child time to accept limits before she discovers that her anticipated dream gift is not under the tree.

5. **Get organized for incoming gifts.** The gifts can become overwhelming if you don't have room for them or if your child can't play with them in an orderly way. Make a plan to rotate toys or clothes and to give some away. *Giving* before *getting* helps your child to appreciate what she has and to think of other children's happiness along with her own.

6. **Make giving as important as receiving.** Children love to give gifts if they choose the gifts they give, and they see the pleasure others feel when opening them.

Every child deserves an abundance of riches. The entitlement-free child learns to look for the personal value of money and gifts. Money can buy a lot of things, but some things are irreplaceable, and some things cannot be bought. The entitlement-free child may not understand intangible values for years to come, but you will see his contentment in everyday, ordinary activities. Help your child learn to find pleasure in the choices he makes. Pleasure comes from people and places; it comes from inside and outside as well as from things. The child with the most toys doesn't win. The child who has the most fun with his toys wins.

11

AN ENTITLEMENT-FREE FUTURE

When you choose entitlement-free parenting, it permeates your daily routines, decisions, and conversations. You weigh immediate gratification against long-term satisfaction, immediate convenience against long-term importance, and immediate reactions against long-term consequences. You also assume that other people's interests are equal to your own, for no other reason than you're in this together.

But there's no way you want to be the only one on a dusty country road while everyone else is drinking champagne in a penthouse. What are you supposed to do when other people are happily giving in, buying up, praising indiscriminately, and looking for a quick fix? Are the entitlement-partiers really that unhappy? The *image* of entitlement is intoxicating—anything and everything you desire is yours for the taking, as soon as you hold out your hand. The entitlement struggle is as timeless as a Greek myth. It's hard to dispute the image of attainable perfection. But you must look behind the promises and think about whether the entitlement dream really can deliver. From Harvard University to *Forbes* magazine, economists and psychologists agree in their assessments of the "happiness" research: more money and more stuff doesn't bring more happiness—once you exceed the poverty level, that is. Money doesn't solve relationship problems. Look at those child stars who seem to have "everything" only to struggle with addiction and public embarrassment. Or look in your own closet. You were ecstatic with that first pair of designer shoes, but does the fifth pair have the same "wow factor"?

CHOOSE WHAT'S BEST FOR YOUR CHILD

Your child's birthright is independence, instead of a fragile dependence on others to make everything perfect around her. Choose entitlement-free parenting because that's what's best for your child. Give your child the confidence that comes from self-control and the ability to solve age-appropriate problems.

WAIT FOR THE MARSHMALLOWS

Consider the famous "marshmallow test" discussed in Daniel Goleman's book *Emotional Intelligence*. A marshmallow was placed on a table in front of four-year-olds who were told they could eat the marshmallow now or get two if they waited for the researcher to return in twenty minutes. The children who waited were happier and more successful in the long run. Good things *do* come to those who wait. The entitlement-free child does get more—but you have to believe that.

CHOOSE TO BELONG

Caring about others and caring about tomorrow create the entitlement-free balance. Children feel safe, strong, and capable when they know they belong to something bigger than themselves and bigger than this moment. The entitlement-free child is connected to others, and she matters to others. Likewise, the experience of living with others in a shared community strengthens who she is. A reciprocal connection, give-and-take, opens the way for a lasting, loving relationship instead of what-you-can-do-for-me-right-now. The child who belongs has a place of value for today and for tomorrow. Sometimes entitlement foot-stamping is rewarded, but in the long run, it destroys genuine mutual concern. Entitlement-free decisions are based upon what works for everyone, not just what works for one child.

THE ENTITLEMENT-FREE FAMILY

Standing apart from the entitlement hype, the entitlement-free family resists the too-good-to-be-true promises of instant gratification. If only a perfect birthday party made for a perfect year, and giving in today made for an easier tomorrow; but that's not the case. If only you could protect your child from heartbreak and insulate her from trouble; but you can't be everywhere, always. The good news is that you can do so much more:

- You can create a refuge in your home.
- You can give your child a place to talk about struggles.
- You can guide your child to constructive action.
- You can help your child learn from her successes and mistakes.
- You can teach your child values that will fortify her.
- You can show your child there's strength in trying.
- You can say no when your child's searching for boundaries.
- You can say, "Not yet" when your child needs more skills or more maturity.
- You can say yes to learning and personal responsibility.
- You can expect much and show your child the steps to achieve it.

The entitlement-free family builds a bridge for each child to make her way into the real world. The bridge begins in the childhood world of magic and make-believe and ends in the adult world of self-control and logic. Parents and children walk back and forth over that bridge thousands of times before the child is ready to go alone. Each day-to-day situation is scaffolding under that bridge to support the entitlement-free child on her way to a unique place in the world. The entitlement-free family shows each child how to maneuver in and out of that world of grown-up expectations until, one day, the child is no longer a child but a person ready for independence.

Problem solving involves risk-taking and a little trial and error. With the help of her family, the entitlement-free child learns problem solving like a marathon runner. She knows she can succeed, because she already has the miles to prove it. Her running shoes are broken in. She's practiced in all kinds of weather and conditions. She can solve problems, day in and day out.

THE ENTITLEMENT-FREE FAMILY

- Makes time in daily routines to think, plan, and discuss
- Promotes curiosity with open-ended discussions of "What else?" and "What if?"
- Examines the situation from other people's perspectives
- Connects feelings and thoughts to choices and actions

Children raised in entitlement-free families become adept problem solvers, because they've watched you for years, learning from your mistakes as well as from their own. In the entitlement-free family, problem solving is fun; it's normal. The more you do it, the easier it is.

THE ENTITLEMENT-FREE FUTURE

An entitlement-free future is a place where honesty, integrity, and communication are possible. The heroes are children and grown-ups who engage one another with mutual respect, working together, whether someone is right or wrong, to find a better way. An entitlement-free community shares a basic principle that different personalities and different needs can coexist without intimidation or power struggles. Conflict is not avoided out of desperation or a fear of lawsuits but rather met openly as an opportunity to redefine what works and what doesn't work.

An entitlement-free community responds to public tantrums the same way a parent responds to an impulsive two-year-old, with a recommendation to start again when emotions are calmer. Businesses and services move beyond patronizing entitlement slogans like "The customer is always right." The entitlement-free community patiently reshapes public transactions and public conversations. Social expectations—what is polite, what is unacceptable—are expressed clearly and up front. People can talk without donning the kid gloves—or the boxing gloves. Respectful honesty is no longer politically incorrect.

Who will make the first move? I will, because I know there's a better alternative. You can too. Start in your home with your youngest child. Start by saying no to intimidation. Don't be afraid of challenging emotions—your own or others'. Get comfortable making mistakes, and get a little smarter every day. The future requires taking a chance—bet on yourself, and bet on your child. Entitlement-free parenting is not settling for less. It's standing up for more.

INDEX

ABOUT THE AUTHOR

photo by Amy Weissman

Karen Deerwester is the owner of Family Time Coaching and Consulting and is a highly respected speaker and consultant for parents and educators. Karen gives parents practical and personal parenting solutions through her one-on-one coaching, weekly classes and seminars, and writing for *South Florida Parenting* magazine, FamilyTimeInc.com, and BlueSuitMom.com. She is also featured regularly on numerous other parenting websites. She has appeared on MSNBC, NBC, and NPR, as well as in *Parents* and *Parenting* magazines. Her other books include *The Playskool Guide to Potty Training* (Sourcebooks, 2008) and *The Potty Training Answer Book* (Sourcebooks, 2007), which won the 2008 NAPPA Gold Award for parenting resources.